DIFFERENCE BETWEEN AN "A" S
+ THEE

I AM NOT FO.
ALLOW FAILURES
DICTATE MY FUTURE!!!

WHAT WE BUILD IN THE SPIRIT.
WE BUILD IN THE NATURAL.
HEBS 11 V 13

MULTIPLICATION

WHAT WILL
YOU
do YOUTH
SEE IT
IN THE
SPIRIT ??

THE PRICE OF
VISION - FRUSTRATION
+
DISS APPOINTMENT

MULTIPLICATION

Inspiration And Tools For Church Planting

NICK KLINKENBERG

Published by: VISION PRINT
contact: nick@visionchurches.com

Cover design: Paul Wayland Lee, www.LeewayCreative.com
Editing and interior layout: Creatively Inspired, LLC, www.CreativelyInspiredLife.com

First edition 2008. Second edition 2017
Printed in New Zealand.

ISBN: 978-0-473-38594-1

I DEDICATE THIS BOOK—

to my wife Karen who has faithfully walked
this crazy journey of church planting with me;

to my children who will see
some of what I have imagined;

to my grandchildren who will see
the reality of multiplication that I have on my heart;
and

to all those who are committed to see
His Kingdom expand and multiply.

ENDORSEMENTS

Nick Klinkenberg has made an invaluable contribution to Christian ministry in New Zealand and beyond for many years. Over these years, he has learned many valuable lessons, which the wise will be eager to heed. I commend Nick and his works to you as being highly beneficial resources for the Christian leader, and all who aspire to usefulness in evangelism, church planting, and Kingdom work.

—Phil Pringle
President, C3 Global

Nick Klinkenberg succinctly delivers the rationale and inspiration for the new move of church planting God is calling forth in the nations in our lifetime. Rather than just chronicle this movement, *Multiplication* is a playbook to coach and equip you to be part of it. Subtract whatever else you were doing, add it to the top of your reading list, and get multiplying!

—Anthony Delaney
Leader of Ivy Churches UK and NewThing Europe

I fully endorse this new version of *Multiplication*. This is a book that gets us back to the key point: saving the world. If we are ever to reach the world, we need new believers who breed new believers, and we need to reach them in different ways. Not just adding to the numbers in each church, but multiplying through new church plants. Using that new life and passion to reach out and start new groups, multiplying each person's effort in these last days will speed up the work and ministry of Jesus Christ to the world.

—Chris Hubbard, MBA, MCGD, Grad Dip ALT.
CEO ATC NZ (Vision College)

Multiplication is a book that is deeply imbedded with the thought that "lost people matter to God," and they can matter to us. After 2,000 years of the Church being in existence, there is still much to do so that those who have never heard will hear. You will be inspired by Nick's expansive and contagious faith, his practical 'how to' strategies, and his conviction the planet needs millions of churches. It's your turn now to start by planting!!

—Ian Green
Executive Director
Proton Foundation, UK

It's interesting that only the human species was commissioned by God to multiply. Echoing these words, this book, *Multiplication*, follows the commanding Word of God: Go and make disciples. In other words, plant churches.

—Dr. Cors Ephraïm, MD
Senior Pastor
Capitol Family Centre, Terneuzen, Nederlands

I've known Nick Klinkenberg for more than 20 years. He's been a church planter, senior pastor, movement leader, and pioneer. Read this book, *Multiplication*, and learn from his lifetime of experience. Even better, you'll catch the fire that burns in his heart.

—Steve Addison, UK
Author, *Pioneering Movements: Leadership That Multiplies Disciples and Churches*

Few have grasped the significance of Church planting as the premiere way of reaching lost people and allowing the gospel to penetrate new people groups. Nick is not a theoretician in the planting of churches but an actual practitioner who has done it in more than simply his home country. The critical elements in this book that make it worth the read and better still the utilization of the information is 2-fold:

1. It is chock full with real-world proven tips and strategies. You don't need to make critical mistakes. There is a road map.

2. He believes that fishing is best done by a net rather than just a hook and line. By this I mean he gives practical help to aid these new churches build into their DNA the ability to be a church plant that

plants another church. This is the biblical pattern. If we are to bear fruit after our kind, the fruit of a new church is another new church. Only with this strategy will we see the multitudes reached quickly for the glory of God.

Multiplication is well worth reading and we will make it a part of our seminary's required reading.

—Robert Orr, PhD, DD
President California State Christian University, USA

Nick Klinkenberg is an incredible mix of both apostolic leader and pastor. So when I am around him, I get both his passion for the cause *and* passion for the people of the cause. Combined together I found this to be explosive—his growing of churches and his consultation to churches.

—Steve Warren
Senior Pastor, C3, Amsterdam, NL

Nick Klinkenberg has a long and impressive track record of fruitful ministry, both within a local church, and across the wider body of Christ. When he speaks (or writes), the wise will listen (or read).

—Steve Burgess, Senior Pastor, South City C3,
Christchurch NZ, Regional Overseer C3 Pacific

Nick has always walked the talk: from the first time we met I've been impressed by his zeal in planting churches. He has rubbed off—we planted a church that went on to plant others. This is an immensely practical book that details how to plant successful churches that plant churches, successfully. Read and be transformed!

—Steve Hirst.
Founding Pastor, C3 Hope Chapel, Hamilton NZ

This revamped version of Nick Klinkenberg's book, *Multiplication*, with new chapters and everything revised is even more excellent than the first one. It encapsulates the deepening of truths and lessons of Nick's own exciting and challenging journey of planting church-planting movements in Europe. Not only is it very inspiring and full of challenging insights, but the Reflection page following each chapter give us opportunity to gain more traction with the powerful message contained in each chapter. If taken seriously, *Multiplication* has the potential to help create much explosive and sustainable impact for the Kingdom of God and help fulfill the Great Commission.

—Graham Davison
Senior Minister, Grace International, Leader of HIM Network
Auckland NZ

In this book, *Multiplication*, Nick has captured the essence of the greatest challenge the Church faces. Planting churches is a critical component in spreading the Good News. And although not everyone can do it, it is vitally important for those who can to get started. Maybe you're not the one to lead the plant, but everyone can be involved. Labourers, prayer warriors, and supporters are all essential for a church plant to succeed. As you read *Multiplication*, you will learn how and why.

—Wayne Swift
National Leader, Apostolic Church
Australia

With 4 decades in Christian ministry and a vast range of experience, the one topic that I think sums up Nick's passion and all he lives for is 'Church Planting'. *Multiplication* is, therefore, a book that he is probably more qualified than anyone to write and one that I believe all leaders should read and allow to shape their future ministry.

—Joel Fryett
Senior Pastor, Hope Chapel NZ
C3 Church Global

Any book that inspires us to look at engaging in new pioneering endeavours is always a winner in my eyes. *Multiplication* does exactly that. The challenge to have a vision to see multiplication take place through church planting endeavours will encourage many. It is an apostolic mandate that will both motivate and challenge individuals and networks to think beyond their present expectations.

—Fraser Hardy
LinkNZ Network

I believe that *Multiplication* is a very important book for everyone to read who is serious about the Great Commission. Nick Klinkenberg speaks from a lot of practical (European!) experience and you will taste that in everything you read. *Multiplication* will challenge, help, and encourage you to plant new churches.

—Christiaan Bakker (MA)
Voorganger Evangelische Gemeente CrOsspoint (Oss, the Netherlands)

I have had the privilege of knowing Nick since his first church plant many years ago, and right through to today, Nick is the ultimate church-planting practitioner, not a theoretician. What you read in *Multiplication* has been tried and tested and proven to be effective and fruitful, and will serve as both a "how to" and a reference book along the journey of planting. As a fellow church planter, I hugely respect Nick for both what he has accomplished in church planting, and as a skilled communicator in the art and work of church planting.

—Lloyd Rankin
National Director, Vineyard Churches
Aotearoa New Zealand

Expect to be excited and disturbed by this book, *Multiplication*. From beginning to end, it makes clear the divine mandate for the church of the Living God and our role in her multiplication. Pastor Nick Klinkenberg draws on many years of experience gathered from Australasia to Europe, and parts in between, to place in our hands a tool which will provoke us to do the works prepared in advance for us to do.

—Philip G. Underwood
Regional overseer Elim churches, USA

In *Multiplication*, Nick Klinkenberg asserts church planting to be "evangelism's most effective, enduring, integrating, and renewable discipline." I love this assertion's vision. He has developed and written for us an inspirational handbook in two equally empowering halves. It is more than a Yes-but-How?-message; it is "Yes, and How?". The chapters engaging the Yes are supported by the appendices empowering the How.

—Revd Dr. John Douglas
Associate pastor, Bethlehem Baptist Church,
Tauranga NZ

Too many churches today are still working with yesterday's models, and this isn't working particularly well. It's very hard to change existing models, but it is time for new models. The most effective way to create new models is to plant new churches. This book, *Multiplication*, written by my good friend, Nick Klinkenberg, is both a practical and timely reminder of this reality.

—Alan Vink
Executive Director, Willow Creek Association, NZ

For over twenty years Nick has been an unrelenting voice championing the cause of church planting, church multiplication, and planting church-planting movements. He has lived this out through a passion and commitment to see this happen, especially in Europe. This book, *Multiplication*, gathers together his insights born of research, networking, and experience on birthing such movements.

—Steve Graham
Principal Equippers College,
Akd NZ

In his book, *Multiplication*, Nick Klinkenberg shares important strategies to help you and your church become a multiplying church. You will also find reflection questions at the end of each chapter to help you process your Multiplication journey, and practical tools to make Multiplication a reality. If have a desire to multiply, you will want to read *Multiplication: Inspiration and Tools For Church Planting.*

—Dave Ferguson
Lead Pastor, Community Christian Church, Lead Visionary –
NewThing, USA

CONTENTS

Acknowledgements 15

Introduction 17

1 Why Plant Churches? 21

2 Multiplication 35

3 Why Start New Networks or New Movements? 43

4 Hindrances in Multiplying Churches and Networks 55

5 Apostolic Leadership is the Key 65

6 Where Have All the Leaders Gone? 73

7 How Do We Develop Leaders? 83

8 The Power of Vision 91

9 Building Our Base 103

10 The Pioneer 107

11 The Main Thing . . . 117

12 Some Say Church Planting Doesn't Work 125

13 The Impossible, Yet Possible, Dream 131

14 Two Key Factors 141

15 Oikos 147

16 Multiplication is in Our DNA 155

Appendices   157

  Appendix A: How to Start New Churches and Multiply Them 159

  Appendix B: What is Church?   177

  Appendix C: Why Plant Churches? . . . More Reasons   181

  Appendix D: Profile of a Church Planter   187

  Appendix E: Church-Centric or Kingdom-Centric?   191

  Appendix F: Ten Universal Elements   197

  Appendix G: The Value and Power of Networks   203

  Appendix H: Having A Multiplication Mindset (MM)   221

About the Author   227

Resources   229

ACKNOWLEDGEMENTS

This book has been over 3 decades in the making. It is only because of large doses of encouragement from others that you have it in your hands. Please allow me to name a few.

- John Douglas, who inspired me in the beginning with the idea that churches must be planted;

- Ron Goulton, who championed the church planting cause;

- The many churches who continually inspire and challenge me towards the greatest cause ever;

- Sarah Chalmers, who perseveringly and generously gave her time and talents towards beginning the rewriting of this second edition;

- Emily Hillery, for her outstanding work in proofing the second edition;

- And of course, my three adult sons who have unknowingly walked part of the journey with me, and my generous and gracious wife, Karen J, who has always encouraged, followed, and spoken into this project, and whose life has never been the same since church planting became my passion . . . thank you, and thank you!

Special thanks to those who worked hard on the first edition: Simon Moetara (theology lecturer and English major) for proofing;

Andrew and Leanne Roughton for typing and editing; Alison Cunnane for editing and proofing; and Rebekah Graham for the original cover.

Finally, I acknowledge God, who by His Holy Spirit has found all sorts of ways to prompt, inspire, disturb, and encourage me to continue to put pen to paper. He is the Alpha and Omega of this simple book, the One it is all about.

May the result of *Multiplication* be the ignition of new networks and movements, with *thousands of churches planted* bringing glory to His name!

INTRODUCTION

Many years ago, in the late 1970s, I remember quite clearly being in a pastor's office and talking about the church he was planting. I met with Pastor John Douglas who had just planted a church in Welcome Bay, Tauranga. We were in the basement of his house where the church was meeting at the time, and I asked a very simple question: "How do you plant a new church? What do you do?" He proceeded to show me various procedures.

I don't remember the rest of the discussion at all. All I know is that something in that brief conversation captivated me that day, and it has mushroomed, growing over the years in its passion and intensity—I was addicted! It was one of those God-defining moments.

To this day I don't know why I was so fascinated by it; maybe my God-given destiny hit me from eternity within the confines of time. Yet without a doubt, it was just one of those very simple yet profound 'God' moments.

Since that time I have had an ache in my being to keep church planting a high priority within the Body of Christ, especially in the Western world. There is an overwhelming need in specific regions of the world, such as Europe, America, Australia, and New Zealand, to plant outposts of Heaven. We desperately need groundbreaking, apostle-type leaders who are able to break through both visible and invisible obstacles. We need people of faith, perseverance, and character. Nations await such leaders to stand up and guide them into the future. This book is written to inspire those revolutionaries to boldly step forward and take ground for Christ.

Three things must be noted

First, every church-health principle needs to be actioned as churches are planted. This book on church-planting churches is not divorced from daily church life. You will find universal, trans-cultural keys that will unlock door after door for multiplying healthy local churches. While theories are discussed, this is also a book for practitioners—those at 'the coal-face.'

Second, this is a dangerous book, for it is written to change the reader and to birth a fire within. It is written to inspire, disturb, and impassion the reader to plant churches. I wanted to sow seeds that will multiply in people; that's where churches that plant churches form, that's where new movements and networks begin—in people's hearts. So as you read I encourage you to receive inspiration and passion for His dreams.

This book is not for the fainthearted. Civilised and domesticated Christianity will be challenged, for it will always be a huge risk to plant an outpost of Heaven.

In C. S. Lewis's famous work, *The Lion, the Witch, and the Wardrobe,*[1] the Pevensie children find themselves in Narnia with news that Aslan the king—a lion!—is on the move. Lucy is somewhat frightened, and asks Beaver, "Is Aslan safe?" (Aslan being a type of Jesus.)

Beaver's reply was, "Oh no, he's not safe, but He's good. He's the King, I tell you!" May I suggest Christianity, security, comfort, and safety don't mix easily? Look at Paul's life, or John the Baptist, or the disciples, or Jesus! John and Jesus were both killed by the time they were 34! Paul and the disciples had uncomfortable lives. Safety, security, comfort, and church planting don't mix!

---

[1] Lewis, C.S. *The Lion, the Witch, and the Wardrobe* (London: Harper Collins Publishers Ltd., 2001), p. 89.

Third. It's fantastic for a church to plant another church! But I have come to a scary, exciting conviction while on this journey of church planting, that God, indeed, wants multiplication. Not only planting one tree, but a forest—an orchard. In fact, forests *and* orchards.

If we are serious about reaching our world, we need new movements and networks. Igniting church-planting movements has captivated me. Let it captivate you and see what God will do.

As Willow Creeks' Senior Pastor, Bill Hybels' has succinctly said:

> *The church is the hope of the world, and its future rests in the hands of its leaders.[2]*

Jesus Himself uses the highest metaphor that could be used when He calls the church His Bride. The church is not some offbeat society or obscure gathering that meets simply to keep people busy and active. *His church is plan A and there is absolutely no plan B.[3]* It is a matter of life and death. We have the amazing privilege of an invitation by the Creator Himself to begin these supernatural communities of faith. What an adventure!

My life Scripture, which I've paraphrased, is based on Ephesians 3:20-21:

> *God is able to do exceeding abundantly beyond all that we ask, think, or imagine, according to the power that works within us; to Him be the glory in the church and in Christ Jesus, to all generations, forever and ever, amen!"*

What are you asking for with regards to your church? What are you imagining for your church?

---

[2] Hybels, Bill. *Courageous Leadership* (Grand Rapids, Michigan: Zondervan, 2002), p. 27.

[3] See Eph. 1 and 3 in *The Message.*

God is able to do it—and much, much more!

1 WHY PLANT CHURCHES?

Many people have a problem with church . . . so take church to them.

Imagine being able to one day say we are planting one church for every day of the year . . . sometimes two.

I look forward to seeing that taking place in the Western world. George Hunter would say, "What apostolic confidence these people had!" I believe it can happen again. It must happen if we are serious about reaching our world!

In 1881, C.C. McCabe sat on a train heading towards the Pacific Northwest of the United States. In a few days he would be heading the planning and fundraising for the planting of Methodist churches over much of Oregon, Idaho, and Washington. The Methodist Church was starting more than one new congregation a day; some months they averaged two churches a day.

An article in McCabe's morning newspaper featured a speech delivered in Chicago by Robert G. Ingersoll, the famous agnostic philosopher, to a convention of the Freethinkers Association of America. Ingersoll's speech declared:

The churches are dying out all over the earth; they are struck with death.

When the train stopped at the next town, McCabe sent a telegram to Ingersoll who was still at the convention.

Dear Robert:

All hail the power of Jesus' name! We are building more than one Methodist church for every day in the year and propose to make it two a day!

—C.C. McCabe

Word about the telegram leaked out and somebody wrote a folk hymn, in true Methodist tradition, that was sung throughout the Pacific Northwest at preaching missions, camp meetings, and Sunday services.

"The infidels, a motley band,
In council met and said:
The churches are dying across the land
And soon will all be dead."
When suddenly a message came
And struck them with dismay,
'All hail the power of Jesus' name,
We're building two a day!'
"We're building two a day, dear Bob,
We're building two a day!
All hail the power of Jesus' name,
We're building two a day."[4]

Can it happen again? Absolutely. There is more information and resources in our day than ever before.

The big question is this: "Are there people with the apostolic

---

[4] Excerpts from George G. Hunter's book, *To Spread the Power* (Abington Press, 1987), pp. 19 to 20.

confidence that is needed?" It begins with men and women who have confident and persevering faith, a resolve in God and His Word, saying yes to Him.

Don't we have enough churches? From a superficial overview of Western nations, we seem to have churches on every corner.

> *The single most effective method for fulfilling the Great Commission that Jesus gave to us is to plant new churches. Two thousand years of Christian history have proven that new churches grow faster, and reach more people, than established churches. The growth on any plant is always on the newest branches.*[5]

—Rick Warren

Mission leaders worldwide agree that *church planting is the best long-term evangelistic method under Heaven.*

France has approximately 37,500 towns, cities, or villages; of these, 34,000 do not have one evangelical church. I can take you to many, many towns and villages in South Holland, Belgium, and Spain that have no evangelical congregations. In Belgium, a large church is 80 people. There are countless towns and villages that have no evangelical congregations, and even in the cities there is so much room for new churches to be planted. In France, Belgium, Spain, and South Holland, less that half a percent are Christian. From my time in these countries, and talking to top Christian leaders, a half of the half-percent are nationals only. There is a lot of work to do.

America, with its countless bookshops, radio, and TV stations and programmes, and so many excellent model churches, still has 200 million people unreached. As of November 2016, there are 325 millon people in the USA.[6]

---

[5] Stetzer & Bird. *Viral Churches* (Jossey-Bass, 2010.), p. 11.
[6] Sourced from worldometers.info/world-population/us-population

In fact, research done in 1993 showed that 57 denominations representing 61% of all Christian churches in the United States had seen increase of just over one tenth of one percent between 1980 and 1992.[7]

New research says the primary mainline denominations, such as the Christian Church (Disciples of Christ), Reformed Church in America, United Church of Christ (Congregationalist), Episcopal Church, Presbyterian Church (USA), United Methodist Church, Evangelical Lutheran Church in America, and American Baptist churches, had all seriously declined in membership from 1970 till 2012.

Every one of the following primary non-mainline denominations has increased in membership since the 1960s, some by large percentages. These are: Church of God in Christ, Presbyterian Church in America (founded 1974), Evangelical Free Church of America, Assemblies of God, African Methodist Episcopal Church, Southern Baptist Convention, and the Lutheran Church-Missouri Synod.[8]

> **Evangelism is completed when people are serving God in His church.**

Some would say that the American church is being redefined. Cultural Christians are becoming less and less, and people are often attending only 2-3 times a month, not every week. There are some who are congregational Christians; they are what we would call nominal—meaning they grew up in the church, married there perhaps, and may even visit occasionally.[9]

---

[7] Montgomery, J. *Then the End Will Come* (Pasadena: William Carey Library, 1997), p. 6.
[8] Sourced from thegospelcoalition.org/article/factchecker-are-all-christian-denominations-in-decline
[9] Sourced from christianitytoday.com/edstetzer/2013/october/state-of-american-church

Other research[10] talks about the decline of the American church. But Dr. Aubrey Malphurs notes:

Church planting needs to take place.

He goes onto say:

Healthy churches are normally the incubators of church plants. Vibrant, healthy churches produce healthy, vibrant offspring. This will begin the reversal of the declining and plateauing patterns we see within the Church today.

Warren Bird says in Rev Magazine:[11]

An important shift happened in recent years. After decades of net decline, more U.S. churches are being started each year, approximately 4,000, than those being closed each year, approximately 3,500.[12]

In the USA, church planting is now becoming a focus; it's even becoming the thing to do.

Today energy and enthusiasm about church planting in North America is at an unprecedented high.[13]

There are more church planting resources, books, funding, potential planters, and sponsor churches than at any other time in history. There are more courses being offered through conferences and seminars than ever before. "Exponential",[14] a conference focussed solely on church planting, draws thousands each year in the USA.

This is all so exciting and needs to happen. Yet there are millions who still need to know Christ and be discipled. ***The focus is not who's***

---

[10] Sourced from: malphursgroup.com/state-of-the-american-church-plateaued-declining

[11] revmagazine.com, July-Aug, 2007.

[12] Ibid., Warren and Bird. *Viral Churches,* p. 1.

[13] Ibid., p. 32.

[14] See their website Exponential.org.

in the fold, but those outside of the fold. If there are approximately 320,000 churches in USA[15] with an average attendance of 130 people (75-80% of churches worldwide have 100 or less in attendance), then let's be generous and say there are 42 million Americans in a church community (and we'll add 18 million just in case we missed a few), this would be a total of 60 million people. We still have at least 265 million[16] people who need to follow Jesus and make Him the centre of their lives. It's also interesting to note that one of the fastest growing statistics are of those in the USA (as well as in NZ) who do not want to be affiliated or linked with the church or anything Christian or religious. In addition, 80 percent of churches in the USA are either in decline or have reached a plateau.[17]

In New Zealand, we have 4,000 church buildings, but still have at least three and a half million Kiwis unreached. In the Western side of Europe, there are an estimated 406 million people yet to be reached.[18]

We are losing whole generations.

I don't know about you but the above statistics for me are so disturbing and a very real concern. Millions are going to a hell-bound eternity. There has to be an answer.

If we are to reach these millions and millions of lost people with the limited resources that we have, what method would be the best to employ to see these people come to Christ? What would the biblical model be? What are mission leaders around the world stating as the best way to evangelise?

Let's define evangelism:

> *Evangelism is to so present Jesus Christ in the power*
> *of the Holy Spirit that men (and women) might come*

---

[15] Sourced from http://churchrelevance.com/qa-how-many-us-churches-exist
[16] As of 2016, the USA population was 325 million.
[17] Statistic mentioned by Dave Ferguson at Exponential Conference, Manchester, UK, 2016.
[18] These figures according to 2016 statistics.

> *to trust Him as Saviour and serve Him as Lord in the*
> *fellowship of His church.[19]*

Evangelism is completed when people are serving God in His church.

In Matthew 28:19-20, Jesus said:

> *Go therefore and make disciples of all nations,*
> *baptizing them in the name of the Father and the Son*
> *and the Holy Spirit, teaching them to observe all that*
> *I commanded you (NKJV).*

So we see that evangelism is going, making disciples, baptising, and teaching people to GO.

Where better for this to be fulfilled than the local church?

In his book, *Breaking the Stained Glass Barrier*, David Womack writes:

> *There is only one way the Great Commission can be*
> *fulfilled, and that is by establishing Gospel-preaching*
> *congregations in every community on the face of the*
> *earth.[20]*

Dr. Jim Montgomery concurs, stating:

> *A number of leading missiologists are saying that the*
> *most direct way to complete the Great Commission*
> *is to fill the earth—rural areas, cities, countries,*
> *regions, and people-groups—with evangelical*
> *congregations.[21]*

---

[19] Church of England. Archbishop's Third Committee of Inquiry, *The Evangelistic work of the Church: being the Report of the Archbishop's Third Committee of Inquiry* (London: S.P.C.K., 1918).

[20] Womack, D. *Breaking the Stained Glass Barrier* (New York: Harper & Row, 1973).

[21] "Principles and Practices of DAWN: A Growing Movement for World Evangelization"; a paper by Dr. James Montgomery, founder of DAWN Ministries.

In church-growth thinking there are many evangelistic methods. Principles remain constant but methods vary according to culture and circumstances. Yet there is one method that has superseded them all, which Peter Wagner calls the "best evangelistic method under Heaven": church planting.

In his book, *Spreading the Fire*, Wagner writes:

> *The most concrete, lasting form of ministry in Acts is church planting.*[22]

In a later volume, he goes on to say:

> *No missiological principle is more important than saturation church planting.*[23]

Dr. Ralph Winter also provides helpful comments in this area:

> *The extensive activity of starting new congregations, the care and feeding of (new) congregations is thus to me the central activity to which all evangelistic methods must be bent.*[24]

The reason we begin new churches is for harvest!

The best way to reach this world for Christ, is to plant more churches. It's all about harvest. It's about planting outposts of Heaven.

Dr. Larry Lewis, one-time president of the Southern Baptist Home Mission, expressed it this way:

> *The hardest job in your life will be to convince me that we already have too many churches. When our research department tells me that we now have 172 million lost people in America, that we have more unsaved and unchurched than we've ever had in*

---

[22] Wagner, C.P. *Spreading the Fire* (Ventura, CA: Regal books, 1994). p. 60.
[23] Wagner, C.P. *Blazing the Way* (Ventura, CA: Regal books, 1995), p. 48.
[24] Montgomery, Jim. *The Principles and Practices of DAWN: A Growing Movement For World Evangelism, (San Jose, CA, Dawn Ministries, 2nd ed.), pp. 6-8.

the history of this nation, you'll have a hard time convincing me that the day is over when we need to begin new congregations. [25] [26]

Most countries—particularly Western nations—have huge populations who don't have a clue who Christ is. There are millions of people—even in a small country like New Zealand!—who have no personal relationship with Him. Let me quote from Wagner: "I am convinced that the best evangelistic method under Heaven is the planting of churches"—dynamic communities of faith where believers do life together and reach their world for Christ.[27]

It disturbs me that many of the people in our communities are bound for a Christless eternity—Hell. We must reach them. It is a command, an imperative. Jesus tells us to do it; there is no option.

If your church is not in the business of planting churches, the question is not, "Why should we be involved?" but "How can we do it to the best of our ability?"

New congregations are the life-blood and cutting edge of any movement. Each new church is a seed planted that yields 30-fold, 60-fold, or 100-fold increase.

It needs to be noted that every church health/growth principle is realised and needed in church planting.

---

[25] Montgomery, Jim. DAWN Report, #13 (Colorado Springs: Dawn Ministries, 1991), p. 1.

[26] Note: 172 million has grown to 265 million.

[27] I will expand on this more later.

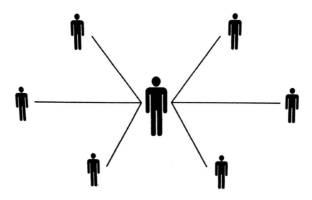

DIAGRAM 1: New convert(s) outreach

Every time a new cluster of converts gathers together in an unchurched neighbourhood or village, there is opportunity to reach out to friends, relatives, and other contacts.

By the way, think about beginning something in the home of the new convert as a starting point. Many people have a problem with church, but not with spiritual things. They may not find it easy to go to a church, and that's why taking church to them is so important. Ask the new convert to bring as many friends as they want to a gathering in their home; speak to them about who Jesus is, and answer their questions regarding Christianity. Offer to pray for those who have needs. It may just be the beginnings of a new church.

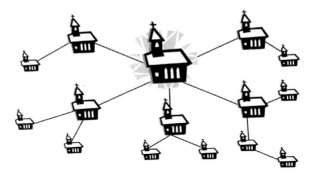

DIAGRAM 2: Church planting new churches

A new convert still has close ties and considerable influence with unbelievers, those who are relatives, neighbours, people in their work environment, sports clubs, etc. It is God's key to the natural and rapid spread of the Good News. He wants us to go into the neighbourhoods of the world.[28]

The movements that grow most rapidly are usually ones that put great emphasis on church multiplication.

Montgomery saw the truth of this in his studies of the church in Guatemala. One denomination, the Principe de Paz (Prince of Peace) is a good illustration. It was the passion of its founder, José Muñoz, to multiply congregations. He constantly challenged his people to reach out to new *barrios*.[29]

"The mission of the church," he said, "is to plant other churches." He repeatedly urged his pastors to plant one new church every year.

---

[28] See Chapter 15.
[29] Spanish for "neighbourhoods".

The result was that in just 27 years, the denomination grew from nothing to become one of the largest denominations in the country—larger than many that had been around a lot longer.

> *When church planting rates soared, membership growth soared. When church planting was neglected, church growth rates declined.*[30]

When we lose our vision for the Great Commission, we not only move into remission as individuals, but also as churches, and it follows that whole movements begin to decline. After many decades of thinking, discussion, prayer, talking to church leaders, and observing movements, I believe every church must be fully engaged in some way in church planting with a structure in place to sustain its momentum.

As I speak on this subject of church planting, I have found there is a very real desire to be involved, but many feel they are unable. I like to encourage every person to find their unique role in this task.

One day, I was speaking in a church that was passionate about planting churches. After the meeting a young mum came up to me and was so desirous to get involved in planting churches, but felt frustrated because she was not only a mum and wife, she and her husband also worked fulltime as medical doctors. They were very busy, but also very influential people. Heartbroken, she felt it was hopeless to think about any personal involvement in church planting.

I said to her, "You could be involved in church planting tomorrow if you wanted."

Stunned she asked, "How?"

I said, "You have the ability to command large dollars into your home, so why not set aside a certain amount of money in a church planting account? Let it grow over the year, or years, and when your church is about to plant, you have finances to give to bless the planting team or the leader of your church to give to the plant."

---

[30] Montgomery, J. *Dawn 2000: 7 Million Churches to Go* (Pasadena: William Carey Library, 1989), p. 17.

Her eyes lit up. I thought, *We have just released finances into the harvest!*

At the conference, Exponential Manchester 2016, Dave Ferguson gave three examples of how you can have a multiplying church.

1. **Everyone have a disciple or an apprentice.** If you have a role in your church, who are you apprenticing? Even if you don't have a role, who are you getting alongside and discipling? (I will address this more in later chapters.)

2. **Being a multiplying church is not about how large it is, it's about leader-readiness.** If you have a church of 50-60 people and you have a leader who is ready to plant a church, then you are able to strategically plant another church with purpose.

3. **A multiplying church necessitates commissioning or ordaining EVERY Christ follower.** What empowerment that would release in a congregation for the Kingdom.

These are just a few ideas, but there are many ways one can be involved in planting a church.

REFLECTION

1. After reading this chapter, why do you think we need to plant more churches?[31] What are you able to do about it?

_____

_____

_____

2. Ponder the author's final question: "How can your church be involved in church planting?" (i.e., reaching the lost).

_____

_____

_____

3. What is God saying to you regarding church planting?

_____

_____

_____

---

[31] See Appendix C for more reasons why churches need to be planted.

2 MULTIPLICATION

I find myself speaking in various leaders' meetings and environments about Multiplication. I wonder if we, as church leaders in the West, have been subtly and innocently sidelined towards being **addicted to addition**. I have a conviction that God wants to multiply His church, not simply add to it.

Look at Jesus' call to Simon Peter and the disciples—telling them that He would make them fishers of people[32]—it was an invitation to partner with others. It was also an offer to the purpose of making them partners with Him in "fishing" for people, as well as a call to follow Him. But I have only recently seen the huge backstory to this passage of Scripture. It would have been a miracle to catch even 10 or 20 fish at that time of day. These were professional fishermen who knew the lake and its environs. To catch any fish at that time of day would have been an amazing miracle. But Jesus asks them to launch out into the deep and let down the nets. They caught so many fish that day, the nets began to break (and note that it was *nets*, not simply a single net). Also, both boats were so full of fish they were in danger of sinking. That's MULTIPLICATION—an out-of-control harvest! That's certainly not simply addition!

I believe Jesus is saying to us today: *Multiplication is My desire*

---

[32] See Luke 5:1-11.

and plan for every disciple and every church. I am convinced Jesus wants us to fish with *nets* (plural). He wants church-planting churches! Let's not allow ourselves to be a cul-de-sac church—a dead-end-street church—a church that doesn't plant churches.

Instead, let's think about planting *forests,* or using *nets,* not simply planting a tree, or fishing with a hook and line.

Here's another way of looking at this: Say we want to multiply car factories. It takes a huge amount of energy and time to make a single car from scratch. But imagine a factory where multiple cars are produced, and not only one factory, but many *factories.*

As you can see I absolutely *believe* in Multiplication as a viable biblical strategy.

Multiplication takes place in a number of ways. Let me explain. I am convinced God wants to multiply people and resources. Let's examine this closer by taking a look at the following Scriptures.

Genesis

> *Then God blessed them, and God said to them, "**Be fruitful and multiply**; fill the earth and subdue it; have dominion over the fish of the sea, over the birds in the air, and over every living thing that moves on the earth."*

> 1:28, NKJV, emphasis added

> *Abram fell facedown, and God said to him, "As for me, this is my covenant with you: You will be the father of many nations. No longer will you be called Abram; your name will be Abraham, for I have made you a father of many nations. **I will make you very fruitful**; I will make nations of you, and kings will come from you. I will establish my covenant as an everlasting covenant between me and you and your descendants after you for the generations to come, to be your God*

> *and the God of your descendants after you. The whole*
> *land of Canaan, where you now reside as a foreigner,*
> *I will give as an everlasting possession to you and*
> *your descendants after you; and I will be their God."*
>
> 17:3-8, emphasis added

> *The angel of the LORD called to Abraham from heaven*
> *a second time and said, "I swear by myself, declares*
> *the LORD, that because you have done this and have*
> *not withheld your son, your only son,* **I will bless you**
> *and* **make your descendants as numerous as the**
> **stars** *in the sky and the <u>sand</u> on the seashore. Your*
> *descendants will take possession of the cities of their*
> *enemies, and through your offspring all the nations*
> *of the earth will be blessed, because you have obeyed*
> *me."*
>
> 22:15-18, emphasis added

It must be noted that because Abraham obeyed God and didn't withhold his only son, blessing came. The result of obedience is always blessing.

These same promises were given to Isaac and Jacob. Because we are heirs of Abraham, God's promise belongs also to us.[33]

Deuteronomy 1:10-11

> *The LORD your God has* **multiplied** *you, and here you*
> *are today, as the stars of heaven in* **multitude**. *May*
> *the LORD God of your fathers make you* **a thousand**
> **times** *more numerous than you are, and bless you as*
> *he has promised you![34]*

I would be pleased if we increased so much that we would be as

---

[33] See Gal. 3:29.
[34] NKJV, emphasis added.

many as the stars in the sky. That's very exciting. But the Scripture goes on and says, *let's multiply this a thousand times!!!*

It's like God doesn't want to add, He wants to multiply! [35]

Mark 4:20

> *Others, like seed sown on good soil, hear the word, accept it, and produce a crop—thirty, sixty, or even a hundred times what was sown.*

Mark 10:29-30

> *"Truly I tell you," Jesus replied, "no one who has left home or brothers or sisters or mother or father or children or fields for me and the gospel will fail to receive a hundred times as much in this present age . . ."*

Matthew 13:8 (NLT)

> *Still other seeds fell on fertile soil, and they produced a crop that was thirty, sixty, and even a hundred times as much as had been planted!*

Matthew 13:31-33 (NLT)

> *The Kingdom of Heaven is like a mustard seed planted in a field. It is the smallest of all seeds, but it becomes the largest of garden plants; it grows into a tree, and birds come and make nests in its branches.*

> *The Kingdom of Heaven is like the yeast a woman used in making bread. Even though she put only a little yeast in three measures of flour, it permeated every part of the dough.*

---

[35] See also Gen. 48:3-4, Lev. 26:3-13, and Josh. 23:9-11.

THE NEW BIG is SMALL !!!

Notice it says, "a little yeast" . . . the "smallest" seed. The smallest and the least multiply. In fact, we see here that the new big is small. Small things multiply more easily.

In John 15 Jesus speaks about "fruit", "more fruit", and "much fruit". Acts 2:47, 6:7, and 9:31 speak about rapid increase in churches and people being discipled.

Look at 2 Corinthians 9:8-11. Here we see multiplication at work in terms of grace, righteousness, generosity, as well as our resources.

> *And **God is able to bless you abundantly**, so that in all things at all times, having all that you need, **you will abound** in every good work. As it is written: "They have freely scattered their gifts to the poor; their righteousness endures forever." Now he who supplies seed to the sower and bread for food will also supply and **increase** your store of seed and will **enlarge** the harvest of your righteousness. **You will be enriched in every way** so that you can be generous on every occasion, and through us your generosity will result in thanksgiving to God.*

(emphasis added)

And my life verse:

> *Now to Him who is able to do exceedingly abundantly above all we ask or think, according to the power that works in us, to Him be glory in the church by Christ Jesus to all generations, forever and ever. Amen.*

Ephesians 3:20-21, NKJV

What are you asking God for? What are you thinking about? What are you imagining? This verse clearly states that God is able to surpass your wildest dreams! This is mind blowing!

WE LiKE To CONTROL.
HE WANTS us To TRUST.

The devil comes to steal, kill, and destroy. He does more than subtract; he divides. But Jesus comes to give us abundant life![36]

I look forward to the day when my European church leaders tell me that a church or churches have been planted out of our network in a city or region in Europe, and we are just catching up with the news that a few new churches have been planted. Or here's a mind-blowing thought: a new network/movement has begun and we are simply hearing the news about it. Imagine that. I look forward to that day. For me, that's divinely out of control.
That's multiplication.

Here's another thought: We can count the apples on an apple tree, but it's difficult to count the seeds on an apple tree. May I suggest that the true fruit of another apple tree is *not* another apple, but another tree! No one knows how many seeds are on an apple tree. Those seeds, if planted, result in trees, hundreds of them. And no one knows how many apples are in one apple seed.

In every apple there is an orchard.

Over the years it would be thousands! That's nature displaying the principle of multiplication. Missilogist Donald McGavran once said:

X *In every apple there is an orchard.* X

If nature can do this, surely with God we are able to see multiplication in our lives and churches.

Perhaps you have heard the story of the inventor of chess, who was given one free wish by the king of India as a reward. As a most modest reward he wished just for one grain of rice on the first square of the chess board, two on the second square, four on the third, eight

---

[36] See John 10:10.

on the forth and so on—doubling it every time. The king, who had initially smiled thinking that he would get off lightly, simply could not grant the wish. He would have to produce 2,223,372,036,000,000,000 kernels, or 153 billion tons of rice—more than the world harvest for the next thousand years![37]

This story highlights a key motivation for planting church-planting churches. When we plant we can sometimes forget the impact one church can make. If that one church can go on multiplying itself many times over, it will reach far beyond even its local boundaries to impact the world. Creating new churches is the best means of evangelising the nations.

So let's pursue planting churches that plant churches with a passion—focussing most of our resources on what I believe to be the most effective form of missions this world has ever seen!

Heirs of Abraham -
In you is multiplication !!!

The closer we get to
God the
more
we understand
His Heart !!!

---

[37] "Planting the Kingdom," from the Australian World Vision paper, Grid. 2000, 1-5. Alan Hirsch, Network Director, Forge Mission Training Network and Executive Director.

REFLECTION

1. What does Multiplication mean for you?

_____

_____

_____

2. Where do you need to adjust and see Multiplication in your life and church?

_____

_____

_____

3. If you were to go to the theater of your imagination and think about Multiplication, where would your imagination take you?

_____

_____

_____

3 WHY START NEW NETWORKS OR NEW MOVEMENTS?

The healthiest churches are those who reproduce.[38]

We have already talked in the first chapter about how the Methodists in the late 1800s were planting one church a day, sometimes two!

A few years ago I had the privilege to travel to Chennai, India, and met Dr. R. (Bobby) Gupta, the President of Hindustan Bible Institute. Now let's go back some 26 years earlier (that's the '80s, and yeah, I was around then!) where I first met Bobby Gupta at a church-planting forum in London. I remember that day well. He spoke about his Hindustan Bible Institute (HBI), training leaders to begin new churches.[39] The students fully graduate when they have planted a church or were part of a team that planted. It was so exciting when I first heard about it, and I've remembered the meeting ever since.

So now, fast-forward 26 years to February 2013 in Chennai and I met him again at the HBI. We ended up talking nonstop for a few

---

[38] According to a national research project called FACT2008.
[39] HBI began in 1952.

hours on church planting movements. It was exciting to hear what has happened. In the past three decades, over 7,000 churches had been planted! Included in this were new movements that are self-sustaining and multiplying.

Bobby Gupta gives a very clear call to the church:

Unless the church focuses on the task of making disciples and planting churches, we will not fulfill the mission of God for our generation.

He goes on to say:

God's mission for the church is to make disciples of the nations, and God insists on accomplishing that mission through us.

As I left the building that day, I noticed the huge board in the foyer of the Bible Training Centre, which read:

To give every Indian an opportunity to hear, understand, and respond to the Gospel, and be discipled into communities of believers, so that we will see a dynamic transformational church in every village, colony, town, and city of India, and beyond.

Building Transformational Leaders to Disciple the Nations.

Wow! May I suggest . . . that's called Multiplication.

In 2015, and again in 2016, I had the privilege to meet Ying Kai, missionary to Asia. He has seen over 2 million people water baptised and 150,000 churches planted! That's Multiplication. I realise this is happening in a very Gospel-responsive nation. But if we are serious about reaching the West for Christ, I am convinced we need new networks and movements to accommodate such results.

After hearing Ying Kai speak and then meeting him personally, I went to a different seminar on the pre-launch of a new Western-style church. These leaders talked about their building, the huge financial commitment for the plant (at least two paid staff and a very qualified lead pastor), plus equipment, music, and host teams, etc. As much as I applaud them for planting a church, I think it will be very difficult to multiply this kind of model.

In contrast, Ying Kai had no finances, no seminary-trained leader (yet their leaders are highly discipled), no buildings, and no control—he was simply releasing people into the harvest and giving them the tools to disciple and plant. Also, the number in each church was small as is necessary in a restrictive and politically repressive nation. The fact is, **small churches multiply more easily.** Also, there was a high value of discipleship. **Discipleship and multiplication go together.** A push-bike will not move forward without two pedals. Discipleship and multiplication are like the two pedals. Multiplication without discipleship is unsustainable. We'll talk more about this, and also church size, later.

> I believe God's plan is that churches plant churches that multiply themselves.

The difference between an elephant and a rabbit is another example of Multiplication. In church plants, small is the new big.

Elephants:

- Only fertile four times a year
- Have one baby per pregnancy
- Twenty-two-month gestation period
- Sexual maturity at 18 years
- Maximum growth potential in three years: two to three

Rabbits:

- Almost continuously fertile
- Average of seven babies per pregnancy
- One-month gestation period
- Sexual maturity at four months
- Maximum growth potential in three years: two to 476 million

That's multiplication.

I want to suggest two modifications (in bold print) to the well-known C.P. Wagner quote:

> *The single most effective **long term** evangelistic method under heaven is planting new churches **that plant new churches.***

> *I believe God's plan is that churches plant churches; they multiply themselves.*

Among protestant congregations surveyed, those whose leadership spent the most time recruiting and training leaders were the healthiest. Similar results came from leaders who promoted a clear vision and emphasized evangelism. The massive survey factored in results from more than 2,000 random Protestant congregations.[40]

Stetzer and Bird say:

> *For years, most Bible teachers have referred to Paul's travels as his "missionary journeys." We prefer to call them Paul's "church planting journeys."[41]*

I am convinced church planting is not a theory, trend, programme, or the latest fad. Church planting is the dominant method of evangelism in the book of Acts, and the key to spreading the Gospel.

---

[40] Ibid., Stetzer & Bird. *Viral Churches*, p. 31.
[41] Ibid., p. 43.

What about churches planting churches that plant churches? Instead of churches only making disciples, what about disciples reproducing themselves . . . disciples multiplying churches? Imagine if churches that were planted were *planted already pregnant* with the next church. *I wonder how many movements a disciple could plant?* Radical!

After all, we are commanded to 'disciple nations'.[42] We must think past addition. The church planting equation $3 + 3 + 3 = 9$ is wonderful, and better than nothing, but what about $3 \times 3 \times 3 = 27$? We need to think in terms of Multiplication. Ralf Moore says:

> *It's time to stop counting converts and begin counting congregations.*[43]

Imagine churches that were birthed pregnant. They had in their DNA when they began that they were going to continue planting churches. What a great purpose for every new church!

Like I said earlier, too many churches are becoming a cul-de-sac church—a church that doesn't plant another church.

To effectively reach the West, we *must* strategically begin new networks or movements. We need churches of all shapes and sizes meeting in all sorts of different places: from homes to halls, cafés to concert chambers, classrooms to school rooms, university campuses to theatres.

If we don't strategise for this, Europe—in fact, the world—will not be reached. It is necessary that we start in the influential cities. But what about the thousands and thousands of small towns and villages, as we see in Europe? Even larger cities are many small villages merging into one.

Churches reach a certain size because of many factors, but usually two: the leadership capacity of the leader, and of course, the size of the

---

[42] See Matt. 23:19-20.
[43] FACT2008, Hartford Institute for Religion Research, hartfordinstitute.org.

city, town, or village. This does not always need to be an issue.

Let's find leaders of 1,000s, 100s, 50s, and 10s, and network together to support, encourage, and resource them, so that life-giving, vibrant, reproducible churches are the result. It is an interesting fact that 75% of leaders have the capacity to lead 100 people or less. (Moses' father-in-law, Jethro, recommended this concept to him.) It is also interesting to note that even today, 75-80% of churches worldwide are around 100 or less in attendance!

I heard C.P. Wagner give a lecture when he was in New Zealand. He said:

> God must love the small church; He made so many
> of them.

Maybe there is a reason for this. Could it be that it is easier for small groups to multiply, and it's easier to find leaders of 100 or less than 1,000?

Imagine 6 small villages, some with 2,500 people to 5,000 people within a radius of 19 kilometres. Usually one village is unable to sustain a church, buy buildings, etc. I realise there are exceptions, of course. But remember, we are talking about the rapid multiplication of new churches! So one congregation has 48 people, another grows to 26 people, three others are around 45 people, and one is 75 people—284 people in total.

They are each too small to bring in guest speakers, host special seminars or courses, or really serve their village with a Bible training school providing expertise. They certainly don't have the finance to buy a building or begin new congregations. Many may not have the musicians or drama teams to put on special events throughout the year. But partnering together, they can do so much! They can put on excellent events, have guest speakers, host courses or training seminars to serve the villages, plus start new churches!

Let me go further—this MUST happen if we are to reach Europe!

Coordinating in this way will form new networks and movements. In fact, it will be these **networks and movements that will start other movements!** Imagine that!

As always, good leadership is a huge key to its success—in this case, apostleship. We will address this in the next chapter.

What is a church planting movement?

According to Garrison:

> *A church planting movement is a rapid and multiplicative increase of indigenous church planting churches within a given people group or population segment.*[44]

History would tend to suggest that after a period of time movements which were once vibrant and dynamic in their purpose, end up in maintenance mode or in decline. It's simply the nature of organisations. A very small number do indeed continue to grow, but these seem to be the exception rather than the rule.

I am convinced that **we need to start church planting movements that start new church planting movements.**

Many movements begin with a dream or a vision. This, as we know, seldom happens in a group. A vision usually takes place in and through a person. Then a movement is birthed, and a group is formed around that vision.

For example, Florence Nightingale birthed a movement as she saw the need for nurses. William Booth birthed a church movement focussed on his passion to reach the poor. John Wesley birthed Methodism.

In our time, Demos Shakarian founded Full Gospel Business Men's Fellowship International, which impacted many nations. He had

---

[44] Garrison, David. *Church Planting Movements; How God is Redeeming a Lost World* (Richmond, VA: Wigtake resources, 2003).

a passion for reaching businessmen for Jesus. Philip Pringle birthed the Christian City Church (C3) Movement. Brian Houston has birthed the Hillsong Movement. John Wimber began the Vineyard Movement. Bill Hybels has birthed Willow Creek, which is a movement. What about YWAM, World Vision, Tear Fund, IHOP,[45] Bethel Church, and Jesus Culture? These are just a few. There are so many more.

In fact, some of the 'movement birthers' didn't purposely aim to plant or birth a movement; rather they saw a need and sought to meet it. Imagine if movements could be birthed strategically.

As small groups are a principle for a church to continue to grow— and churches need to continually plant in order for a movement to grow—I am convinced movements need to be planted if we are serious about reaching nations for Christ. **We need many more movements!**

Each church has a unique DNA—a culture of its own. As Ford points out:

> *Each church has a unique makeup that's essential to its life, health, and future.*[46]

The larger a church becomes, and the longer it has existed, the more difficult and challenging it is to change the culture of that church. As this is the case in a church, so it applies to a movement. There is a culture, a purpose, a DNA in a movement of churches. This is very hard to change, and if it *was* possible, would take much time, energy, and focussed effort. It would be simpler to begin another movement. In fact, why should a movement change, if it is indeed meeting a need? Or perhaps its time has come to an end as it has fulfilled its mandate.

In his book, *Churchquake*, C. Peter Wagner states that his 'best guess' is that most apostles[47] can handle up to fifty churches fairly

---

[45] International House of Prayer, Kansas City, KS.

[46] Ford, Kevin G. "Leaders Insight: Your Church's DNA," Leadership Newsletter, July 23, 2007.

[47] The primary responsibility of apostles is to release people for harvest. Because they will more than likely build networks of ministries that release people into harvest, building apostolic networks is not the primary role of apostleship. Paul is a great model of this (see Rom. 1:5; Acts 9:15).

well.[48] Few could handle as many as 150 without creating some form of bureaucracy in order to make it happen. Wagner also notes that the personality of the apostle is undoubtedly the most important variable, and that experience counts as well, with the apostle being able to handle more churches if they are more seasoned and mature.

So why not continue to plant movements, thereby releasing more apostles who create still further styles and cultures, which in turn will meet different needs? The fact is, not everyone will come to one church in a city of 50,000 people. It takes all sorts of different types of churches to minister to people, and the same could be said of movements. It is really interesting that there doesn't seem to be a set pattern in Scripture of how to run a church. The debate has been discussed for centuries and still continues today. The Baptists believe that they have the right church structure, as do the Assemblies of God . . . and the Presbyterians . . . as do the Anglicans . . . and so on and so forth. I think every one of them is right, for I believe God has left it open for a reason so as to give freedom of expression.

What a wonderful trusting God He is—so creative through us.

So what are the factors of a movement?

If we were to strategically plant a movement of churches, how could this be done? I picked up these thoughts from Ben Wong in a discussion with him; he began a movement of churches in Hong Kong many years ago. Observing movements of today, I believe the following keys apply which are timeless and still apply today.

- **Movements move in the power of the Holy Spirit.** There must be a supernatural dynamic led by the Holy Spirit. The gifts of the Spirit must be exercised regularly.

- **Movements have their own music and style,** e.g., such as the camp meetings of the 19th century, Wesley, the Salvation Army, and more recently, Integrity Music,

---

[48] Wagner, C. Peter. *Churchquake: How the New Apostolic Reformation is Shaking up the Church as We Know It* (Ventura: Regal Books, 1999), pp. 141-152.

Vineyard, Hillsong, IHOP, Bethel/Jesus Culture, and C3[49].

• **Movements have their own publications and resources.** Hillsong, C3, Bethel, and many other movements are examples of this. Their way of doing things is recorded and taught elsewhere.

• **Movements have their own training and education.** Again there is a DNA that is caught and taught. Values and the non-negotiables are caught as well as taught and re-taught. A new generation always needs to be disciplined and trained.

• **A movement affects the community in social work.** Church movements do this. Look at the Salvation Army, Methodist, and Pentecostal movements.[50]

Two factors enhance and prepare a movement's growth

1. Ownership

For ownership of vision to take place, others must incarnate this. The aim is people owning the vision as theirs. The result? The vision carries on through the good times, but also through the difficult and problematic times.

2. Training

Continuing training, mentoring, and discipling must take place. Vision and values must be taught and caught over and over again in varying ways by different people. The 'what' and 'why' are huge factors that need to be emphasized again and again.

---

[49] C3, Sydney, Australia.

[50] See Appendix F for Garrison's, "Ten Universal Elements" present in church planting movements.

REFLECTION

1. How have you been challenged through this chapter?

_____

_____

_____

_____

_____

_____

2. What do you feel God is saying to you or to your church regarding movements?

_____

_____

_____

_____

_____

_____

4 HINDRANCES IN MULTIPLYING CHURCHES AND MOVEMENTS

Let's consider the hindrances in multiplying churches and movements, particularly in Western nations. Let me begin with what I consider to be a *huge* challenge. It's what Hirsch and Ferguson talk about in their prophetically insightful book, *On the Verge: A Journey Into the Apostolic Future of the Church*.[51] They call it the *strategic problem*, and I think they state it profoundly well.

> *Most of our churches believe and act as if modeling on and perfecting the successful contemporary church approach will resolve their problems of mission. But even if they could all become successful megachurches, the vast majority of churches cannot and should not. The financial capital, managerial infrastructure, leadership ability, communication strategies, and amount of artistic talent are huge in megachurches—all making for a model that is not very reproducible.*

---

[51] Hirsch, Alan; Ferguson, Dave. *On the Verge: A Journey Into the Apostolic Future of the Church (Exponential Series)*, (Zondervan, 2011), p. 28

They go on to say:

> *Most of our current practices are simply variations of the same model. This is not to say it's wrong or not used by God. . . . Please don't hear us wrong here. Clearly God uses the contemporary church. It is simply to say it is not sufficient to the increasingly missional challenge now set before us.*

If we are honest with ourselves we realise that this is so true!

Let's move on to the four barriers to multiplying your church or movement. Be warned: This will challenge how we apply leadership in our churches, and the way we do church if true multiplication is to occur.

1. **Professionalism.**

There seems to be a need in Western churches for leaders who have a degree or their Master's. Many leaders feel as though they need to be paid full-time or part-time. Maybe this is hindering the releasing of others into their gifts, and the focus of equipping others to pick up ministry and leadership tasks and responsibilities.

This is not so in countries such as China, India, Thailand, etc. Yet the church is multiplying rapidly there as most are volunteers.

2. **Consumerism.**

The question Western Christians often ask is, "What will this church do for me?" Christianity seems to be about my family, my life, meeting my needs, and developing my ministry. The question should not be, "What can the church do for me?" but rather, "How can I partner with the church to fulfill its God-given mission?"

In countries where there is rapid growth, they ask, "What can I do?", "How can I get involved?", and "Where can I serve?" The results are clearly evident.

3. **Individualism.**

Independence is robbing society of community, and it's hindering, if not stealing, that family-feel from a body of believers. About the church, the writer of Hebrews says:

> *Let us think of ways to motivate one another to acts of love and good works. And let us not neglect our meeting together, as some people do, but encourage one another . . .*

> Hebrews 10:24-25, NLT

When Jesus taught us to pray in Matthew 6 and Luke 11, have you noticed the words, *us, our,* and *we* again and again?

> ***Our** Father in heaven . . . Give **us** this day **our** daily bread*[52] *. . .*

Our Father . . . not *my* Father. In other words, there's enough for you, but also enough so the community around you is resourced.

> *And forgive **us our** sins, for **we** also forgive everyone who is indebted to **us**. And do not lead **us** into temptation, but deliver **us** from the evil one.*[53]

Multiplication and Discipleship walk hand in hand.

The local church is all about family, community, and one another. (The Bible is full of "one anothers"—i.e., the books of Romans, Corinthians, Ephesians, Philippians, Colossians, etc.). The message is clear: supporting, encouraging, looking out for and helping one another is priority. Nowhere does the Bible promote a Christianity of me, myself, and I. The Bible is meant to

---

[52] See Matt. 6:9-13, NKJV, emphasis added.
[53] Luke 11:4, NKJV, emphasis added.

be interpreted in community, for community. Have you ever noticed the many letters written by the apostles were sent to communities, not just to individuals? Note also that the Eastern mindset, from which the Bible was written, was centered around family and community.

4. **Pastoral (the Lead Pastor's) insecurity.**

Everybody experiences insecurity from time to time. But as Christians and leaders, we must understand that our identity is in Christ. Our identity is not in our position, status, wealth, or how clever we are. By the way, it's very easy to say that our identity is in Christ, but be assured this will be tested.

We can actually self-medicate through our leadership. This can happen negatively, and if not watched, becomes intoxicating. We think we are anointed when we are simply adrenalized. If we are not careful, we can so easily lead from a place of control and manipulation.

One of the primary roles of a leader is to release others into their giftings and calling. They may even be much more gifted than us in certain areas. If so, are we secure enough to continue to disciple them? Maybe our role will change and we won't be needed in the same way. Discipling, mentoring, and coaching necessitate that we will eventually give away our ministry roles.

Here are some further questions to check the level of our insecurities.

- How many rules do you have in place for your church? We are not policemen; we are pastors.

- Are you the same at home as you are when preaching?

- If people disagree with you, do you quickly sideline them?[54]

---

[54] I am indebted to Micah Fries, who works with NEW CHURCHES for the inspiration of the above points from a lecture given at the Exponential conference in L.A., October 2015.

One of the big hindrances and blockages to multiplying is the **lack of discipleship. You simply cannot have multiplication without discipleship.**

Bill Easum states:

> *Radical discipleship is both father and mother to any exponential church multiplication movement.*[55]

How would you define discipleship? We may have all kinds of definitions in mind; such as, attend the church service, participate in a small group, and serve somewhere in the church. These are good, but not great. I would suggest these are *results* of discipleship, not discipleship itself. There are many books written on this subject, which is attracting a lot of attention. I believe leaders are realising discipleship has been hugely undervalued and overlooked. Leaders may think that because we attend church and are serving, all is well. We feel that discipleship will simply happen. Not so. I've come to the conclusion that discipleship is severely lacking in many churches.

Discipleship is simply trusting and obeying Jesus.

As Bill Easum says:

> *A radical disciple is someone who believes in Jesus and whose beliefs inform and transform their behaviour.*

What did Jesus do? He called 12 people to be with Him. Eating together in their homes, they observed Jesus as He spoke and ministered to people. He talked to them one-on-one and as a group. He spent time with them, which resulted in their beliefs, their lives, and their behaviour being transformed. Profoundly simple, really. It's so doable, I believe anyone can disciple people.

---

[55] From the "Exponential" website, exponential.org, 20th August 2016, resourcing church planters.

Discipleship is NOT a course, seminar, or programme. It's *being* with people, and talking about life, and addressing issues.

> *Teaching them to obey everything I have commanded you . . .*
>
> Matthew 28:20

Christianity is *not* complicated, nor is discipleship. Simply get beside someone and disciple them! Unfortunately, I think we have made the Christian walk very complicated in the West. There seems to be an overemphasis of courses, seminars, and conferences. (By the way, I love these, but not to the exclusion of discipleship.)

I think the following story is not uncommon. A senior pastor was communicating his vision concerning discipleship, and urged all of his paid staff to go out and find 2-3 people to disciple. After 3 months he asked how they were progressing, but none of them had had the time to pick up on it yet. So he restated his request, "Find 2-3 people, and disciple them." In another 3 months he asked his staff how it was going. None of them had even begun to disciple one person yet! It took another 3-6 months before they were actually discipling someone.

My question is, what are we so busy doing that we don't do what Jesus primarily asked us to do? Were these paid staff leaders hesitant to lose a measure of control? Or maybe they felt discipleship wasn't as important as the area of ministry they were already involved in. Perhaps it was that their role had become who they are and discipling others threaten that. Please understand that I'm not wanting to judge but to understand these issues and their very human responses. Maybe these are some of the reasons why Multiplication isn't happening in the West!

Let me say it again, **Multiplication and Discipleship walk hand in hand!**

Less than 4% of U.S. churches ever reproduce, while over 96%

are consumed in the lust of addition growth.[56]

Todd Wilson goes on to say:

Healthy biblical disciple-making is the key to multiplication. Multiplication is not something we do. Instead, multiplication is the overflow and fruit of disciple-making Jesus' way.

So HOW can we disciple?

Jesus said:

Go . . . disciple . . . teaching them to obey everything I have commanded you . . .

Matthew 28:19:20

The *New Century Version* says, "Teach them to obey everything I have *taught* you . . ."[57]

Let me ask, what has Jesus taught you? What has He shown you? How have you worked through questions and issues in your life? How did you go through crises and not go under?

As you read a passage of Scripture with a person you are discipling, ask 3 questions:

1. What do you think Jesus is saying? (**Observation.**)

2. What do you think He is saying to you? (**Interpretation.**)

3. What will you do about this? In other words, how will you apply this in your life? (**Application.**)

This also works well in a small group setting.

---

[56] Todd Wilson, Exponential Director. (Church planter weekly, December 2016.)

[57] NCV, v. 20, emphasis added.

Another thing you can do is take a book that is relevant to the disciple and read it chapter by chapter; when you meet, discuss it. There are many, many creative ways to disciple.

Discipleship is all about the disciple!

Here are some things to consider and questions to ask as you meet together.

- What are you struggling with?
- Find out what questions they have on their mind that need answers.
- How do you feel your marriage is going on a scale of 1-10? What would make it better?
- How do you feel your prayer life is at the moment? Where would you rate it on a scale of 1-10? How could it improve?
- How are your finances looking? (If they are in debt and can't pay bills, this is a huge discipleship issue and needs to be dealt with. So often these areas are not addressed in practical ways.)
- How are your relationships with your kids?
- What work issues are you dealing with now? How can I most effectively pray for you?

Discipleship is about a relationship with Jesus, but also with others. It includes mentoring and coaching. Yet it's more than that. It's a whole-of-life approach. By the way, as the one discipling, you don't need to be an expert in everything. If the person you're discipling is struggling with budgeting, get some help for them from someone who is good at it and has the time to work it through.

REFLECTION

1. How do you feel about the challenge from Hirsch and Ferguson at the beginning of this chapter?

    _____

    _____

    _____

2. Which of the first 4 hindrances have you seen or experienced?

    _____

    _____

    _____

    _____

3. Have you found any of these hindrances in your life? If so, what can you do about that?

    _____

    _____

    _____

    _____

4. Who are the people you could get beside and disciple? (Name 2-3.)

_____

_____

_____

5. Is someone discipling you? If not, who could you ask?

_____

_____

_____

5 APOSTOLIC LEADERSHIP IS THE KEY!

There are so many resources regarding leadership: seminars, conferences, books, and magazines abound. In saying that, leadership is such a huge factor. It has to be mentioned, especially in this book on church planting. Why? Churches won't be planted if leadership doesn't rise up. [58]

But I want to speak about an aspect of leadership that churches who aim to plant churches will intentionally need to align with and see develop. That is: fathering, or apostleship-type leading. Another term could be an overseer. (From now on I will use the word 'apostle', which includes father, overseer—male and female.)

The New Testament mentions a wide variety of people as apostles, not only the Twelve and Paul. The noun, *apostlos,* was a common word in secular Greek. It appears seventy nine times in the New Testament, mostly in the writings of Luke and Paul. The verb, *apostello,* means, "to send," and frequently "to send with a particular purpose."[59]

---

[58] Leadership is also covered in Chapter 6.
[59] Addison, Steve. *Pioneering Movements*, InterVarsity Press, 2015; pp. 41, 45 gives fuller insight on apostleship.

I believe every church needs an apostle-type leader who is voluntarily given authority. They are there to support and encourage, but also have God-given authority to speak into situations and give firm direction.

> *Jesus used the word apostles to describe a role previously unknown by God's people. The word was taken from the practice of the Phoenicians who colonised new territories by sending a leader to people, who was empowered and authorised to establish the rule and culture of the one who sent them.*[60]

Ephesians 4 states that God has given gifts to His church, one of them being apostles. It is a ministry term, not only a leadership term.

> **To be apostolic is about a commitment to reaching lost people for God.** *It's not about a certain type of church government; it's a commitment and passion to win the lost. When looking at the book of Acts, a key element was in the nature of the church; it was apostolic in the sense that the mission was about reaching the world and every member was equipped to play their part.*[61]

Apostles give shape and direction and are able to wisely build churches. They serve, they do not control or manipulate or demand; they inspire, challenge, review, release people into their ministries, and give direction and support. There is a view that apostles are to be served, or be at the top, with others there to serve them. There is nothing further from the truth. If apostles don't serve, they have no right to lead. Servanthood is the door to apostleship. Paul writes:

---

[60] This is based on a paper presented in 2012 by Tim Jack, past national leader of the Australian Apostolic Church, and the present National leader of the UK Apostolic Church.
[61] Ibid.

66

> *So look at Apollos and me as mere servants of Christ . . .*
>
> 1 Corinthians 4:1, NLT

This text pictures the servant as the under-oarsman; it's a place beneath. Another way to explain this is that of an under-rower. In biblical times, small ships had two or three levels where men were placed in chains and rowed. Paul is saying he is on the bottom level. All the rubbish (use a little imagination here) falls on top of the bottom level rowers.

Paul goes onto say:

> *And stewards of the mysteries of God.*
>
> 1 Corinthians 4:1b, NASB

"Stewards" presents the word picture of giving food out to people, or parcelling out food to grazing animals.

The above shows that apostleship in its truest sense is servanthood, sacrifice—releasing God's people into all that He has for them.

> Apostleship, in its truest sense, is servanthood—sacrifice releasing God's people into all He has for them.

Of course, not every leader is an apostle, but I believe every church needs to be connected to apostleship for the sake of the church and its leaders. Movements and networks are led by apostolic leaders. As you can see, this is so important in the planting of movements and networks.

There are many characteristics of an apostle. This list was put together by Christiaan Bakker for his Master's thesis. This is not the end of the discussion on apostleship, but it is well-researched and goes a long way to describe accurately the gifting of apostleship.[62]

1. Apostles are pioneers. They are future-oriented, break with tradition, think multiplication, take risks; they are faith people. They are also entrepreneurial.

2. Apostles create a context in which Apostles, Prophets, Evangelists, Pastors, and Teachers evolve. They not only think about recognizing leaders, but have the ability to see and call out the other giftings.

3. Apostles are fathers to the churches.[63] Apostles train new leaders; they are the spiritual fathers for them.

4. Apostles found churches. On the basis of Ephesians 2:20, apostles together with prophets are seen as the fundaments of the (local) church. The rediscovery of church planting nowadays is being connected to the apostolic in this sense. Apostles birth things, build, and oversee.

5. Apostles maintain worldwide / regional networks and relations. The apostle works on a trans-local/macro level, where they are responsible for the regional cohesion of local churches within a movement. In this sense, of all the ministries they are furthest removed from the local church. They intervene in crisis situations. Their authority is moral or inspirational.

6. Apostles spread Christianity (or: the reign of God). This happens mainly through church planting. They have an 'external' view; they are focussed on reaching the world.

7. Apostles work in a team. The partnership between apostles and prophets is emphasized here, and also by the fact that Paul mainly worked within a team.

---

[62] A full version is found on visionchurches.com, under "RESOURCES".
[63] See 1 Cor. 4:14-21.

8. Apostles are the guardians of the core and fundamental ideas of the church (theologically). Apostles are the guardians of the church teachings (dogmas) and focus on 'the big picture'. *They are passionate about Matthew 28:19-20. They are harvest-focussed.*[64]

9. Apostles initiate and mobilise movement. Apostles have a catalytic function within God's church; they start a movement and make it accelerate.

10. Apostles have a calling. This seems to be something that is 'present' (like a characteristic), and what can be confirmed through prophetic words. Eventually an apostolic calling has to be confirmed by fruit.

I do like this list as it well researched, broad, yet succinct. While it's implied, I would also add, *apostle-type people are marked by perseverance.*

We have the example of the Apostle of apostles, Jesus.

> *We must understand Jesus' mission to understand our mission today. What did Jesus do in the Gospels? What did Jesus do through His disciples in the book of Acts and the rest of the New Testament?*[65]

Steve Addison identifies six activities that describe what Jesus as an Apostle did as the founder of a missionary movement. I believe these are worth noting. I would suggest the following are a model for apostles today. As you read through this list, relate them to pioneers and apostles today:

1. **Jesus saw the end.** He focussed his ministry on Israel while he prepared his disciples to take the Gospel to the whole world.

2. **Jesus connected with people.** Jesus crossed

---

[64] Note: words in italics are my addition.

[65] Ibid., Addison, *Pioneering Movements*, pp. 39, 40.

whatever boundaries stood in the way and connected with people who were far from God. He sought people of peace, the people God had prepared to reach their community.

3. **Jesus shared the Gospel.** Jesus called people to repent and believe in the good news. His death brought forgiveness of sins and life with God.

4. **Jesus trained disciples.** Jesus called disciples out from among the crowds. He taught them a new way of life.

5. **Jesus gathered communities.** Jesus' disciples were the nucleus of the renewed people of God. He prepared the way for the birth of the first church at Pentecost. As the risen Lord, Jesus continues to build his church.

6. **Jesus multiplied workers.** Jesus trained his disciples to make disciples and launched a global missionary movement.

Who are the apostle-type people you are partnering with? Who are the apostles who know you, believe in you, support you, but can also speak very strongly and with authority into your life and church?

I would agree with C.P. Wagner, that most apostle-type leaders can handle up to 50 churches. Once you get more than 50 churches, some kind of bureaucracy needs to be created to facilitate growth.

He also writes:

> *The personality of the apostle is undoubtedly the most important variable . . . experience counts as well. The more mature and seasoned the apostle, the more churches can be handled.*[66]

---

[66] Ibid., Wagner, *Churchquake!*, pp. 141-152.

My prayer is that you see from this chapter that churches and leaders should never do ministry alone; it's simply too dangerous and tough! This is, again, where apostles come into their own. Every church needs a friend, an overseer, a father, an apostle.

REFLECTION

1. Who are the apostle / father figures in your life?

_____

_____

2. Who is partnering with you?

_____

_____

3. Who can you trust, and who trusts you?

_____

_____

4. Who are you allowing to speak strongly and authoritatively into your life and church, while you listen? Accountability is tested when you disagree with the person. It doesn't mean you blindly do what they say, but you will prayerfully consider it.

_____

_____

5. How would you relate Steve Addison's six activities that describe what Jesus did to our modern times?

_____

_____

Growth in the Local and National Church

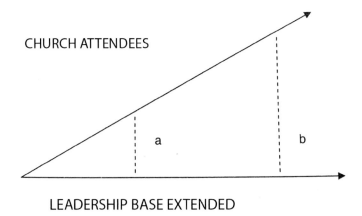

As attendance grows, the leadership base needs to intentionally expand. **The capacity of 'b' is larger than 'a'.** The larger the church attendance, the larger the capacity required of its leaders.

Leadership capacity has the ability to develop. In fact, a larger number of people attending a church demands that leaders grow or the church will not continue to expand. But please don't be discouraged if your capacity is leading a smaller group of 10, 50, or 100 people. A church in this range can easily multiply! **It is not the attendance size that determines when you plant another church, it's whether or not the leader is ready within the existing church to begin a new church.** This is vital for the success of the new plant and the health of the existing church. We really just need to think differently. Consider planting 5 churches of 50 people if you feel your leadership capacity works best in the 50-60 range. The key is to make sure they are networked well. This is why apostolic leaders are needed.

I come from a position that simply believes *everyone* is a leader.[69]

---

[69] Note: This point has been argued and discussed for decades, and the conversation is still alive and well.

We each carry a different capacity to lead, but *all of us* are leaders.

For example, you got out of bed, washed, had breakfast, and arrived in time to be at work today. That's leadership. It's certainly at the lower level, but nevertheless it's still taking leadership of yourself. **The first call of leadership is always to lead oneself!** You cannot lead others effectively if you are unable to lead yourself.

The purpose of leadership is to complete a task or a series of tasks. Leaders want to DO something. They want to reach their community, city, and nation; they want to build a company or start an organisation, and grow it, etc. They need to **do** something!

The function of leadership is a myriad of actions and activities. These functions include planning, empowering, vision casting, setting objectives, strategising, prioritising, finding resources, empowering people, finding and releasing volunteers, building a healthy culture within the organisation, communicating, leading meetings, and much more. In fact, on this topic, John Maxwell says:

Everything rises and falls on leadership.

Leadership Development

We constantly need to extend our base of leadership. We need to ensure that finance is directed towards training programmes and providing opportunities for potential leaders.

If the base of leadership is not developed, the result could be the local church being propped up by the pastor(s) and one or two helpers.

There is a wealth of fantastic leadership resources, conferences, seminars, and courses available for today's leaders that are readily accessible, so I don't want to reinvent the wheel. Get a hold of it all; participate in these leadership training opportunities as much as you can.

Allow me to insert a sidebar on what I see as a major challenge in leadership conversation.

The Priority of the Pastoral and Shepherding side of Leadership

The proliferation of leadership resources over the last three decades is astounding. I applaud it all, and as I've said, I encourage you to get much as you can.

I remember when I went through Bible college back in 1981. There was one leadership magazine that came out of the U.S. once every three months that many of us devoured. At that time, it was about the only journal of its kind on leadership. Things have certainly changed, which is brilliant . . . it really needed to.

> The right to lead comes out of how well we feed. True biblical shepherding and pastoring means leadership is the result.

And yet, it seems the percentage of Christians still hasn't increased overall in NZ. In Europe, the trend is downwards. I'm not sure about other nations, but a brief look at the statistics in the USA suggests no increase. Yes, churches have grown larger and multi-sites are on the increase. And with ever-increasing leadership conversations, resources, and conferences, there are some attitudes that I've seen develop over recent years in corporate leaders of companies and businesses which are also in our churches, but I especially do not like seeing it in Christian leaders. It is the *unhealthy overbalance in leadership and an undervalued aspect of the pastoral, shepherding, and caring-side of ministry.*

The Emphasis is Love

The opposite should be demonstrated in our churches and leadership. *Love people* . . . no matter what. I understand leaders are task-focussed and need a job done well. Amen! But people are never only an end to a means. They are not there solely so the work you want done gets done! No one is perfect, nor will they be perfect. But leaders, really *care* for people; be gentle with them . . . as Jesus would.

Know that people *will* make mistakes—sometimes really bad ones! People will make bad calls; it's just the world we live in. Love them, bring them through, just like Jesus did—and does—with us.

Value Personal Connection

It seems that at a quick glance, communication is at an all-time high. But even with emails, Facebook, Twitter, and all the other platforms of social media, there seems to be a famine of loneliness as people are feeling more isolated like never before. There is just no substitute for personal touch and face-to-face communication. *Could it be we are broadcasting, but not connecting? Perhaps we're connecting, but are we truly hearing? Are we announcing, but not listening? Could we be declaring, yet not discussing?* Simply sending a text message or an email is not truly communicating. An email is read in an impersonal manner. Tone, facial expressions, voice inflection, and empathy cannot be communicated through a text message or a social media post.

Gracious and Caring

The community of faith has an answer, if not *the* answer: shepherds, pastors, and people who really *care* for one another.

Leaders, I admonish you:

> *Be kind . . . tender-hearted . . . forgiving one another . . .*
>
> Ephesians 4:32, NKJV

> *Let your conversation be gracious and attractive . . .*
>
> Colossians 4:6, NLT

When one gets behind the scenes in some leadership situations, the talk about others is often not very uplifting, much less gracious or attractive. Being a leader is not an excuse to be ungracious, nor does it give license for being harsh. Leaders should set the example in forgiveness, graciousness, and kindness.

Shepherd His People

A whole Psalm is dedicated to this idea of shepherding. It's a piece of literature people have recited at special occasions and funerals—Christians and non-Christians alike. In fact, some say it's one of the most famous and recognised passages ever written. I wonder why? Maybe because it shows how much we need shepherding. After all, we are known as sheep! I'm referring to Psalm 23, of course.

> *The Lord is my shepherd . . .*[70]

It doesn't say the Lord is my leader, apostle, prophet, but my Shepherd. Because He is our Shepherd we have everything we need. He gives rest, He leads, renews, guides, takes away fear; He is always with me, protecting and comforting, He prepares food for me, anoints me, my cup always overflows, His goodness and unfailing love pursue me—all because HE is our Shepherd. Wow!! Of course, we also have Psalm 91 and other passages which speak of this shepherding and caring pastoral role.

One of the names of God is Jehovah-Rohi, which means, "Jehovah my Shepherd." In fact, many of the names of God resemble this pastoral attribute, e.g., Jehovah heals, Jehovah my peace, my banner, my provider, He is there, etc.

In John 10:1-17, Jesus speaks of Himself as the Good Shepherd. His sheep recognize His voice; He calls and leads them. Jesus is speaking from an Eastern mindset. In that part of the world a shepherd leads the sheep, whereas in NZ, the shepherd drives the sheep from behind. With the Eastern understanding we see that it's out of the shepherding role leaders lead.

Psalm 23 goes on to say what the good Shepherd does: He gives safety; He gives a rich and satisfying life; He sacrifices His life for the sheep; He brings others into the fold. My thought is this: if you are going to lead well, learn to shepherd and pastor well. As J.C. Douglas once told me:

> *The right to lead comes out of how well we feed.*

---

[70] Ps. 23:1.

Maybe, just maybe, true biblical shepherding and pastoring means leadership is a *result*. Maybe, good leadership is a result of shepherding and caring for people well.

God's Call

Jesus is looking for men and women who will simply say 'yes' to His call. Can you hear God calling you? Remember, it's not our ability; it's our availability.

Millions and millions do not attend any kind of church in Western nations. *Is God calling you to be directly involved in reaching the nations for Christ?*

REFLECTION

1. On a scale of 1-10, what do you feel your level of leadership is? (1 = low, 10 = high)

_____

_____

2. Ask two friends where they feel your leadership level is (scale of 1-10).

_____

_____

3. What would it take to move your leadership level up by 1 or 2 levels? What things would you put in place?

_____

_____

_____

_____

4. How is the pastoral aspect of your leadership? How could you improve in this area?

_____

_____

_____

_____

5. Comment on John Maxwell's quote: "Everything rises and falls on leadership." What does this mean for you?

_____

_____

_____

_____

6. Who are the people who 'tapped you on the shoulder' and challenged you? Who are you tapping on the shoulder? By the way, don't look for the perfect people; look for those with a heart to serve and a teachable attitude. Skill can be taught; attitude is caught.

_____

_____

_____

_____

_____

_____

_____

7 HOW DO WE DEVELOP LEADERS?

George Whitfield saw great revival in the USA. He said of his converts:

My converts are like a rope of sand.

On the other hand, when we look at the generation after John Wesley's death, the Methodist movement began more churches than when he was alive.

To do anything, we need leaders.

American church growth consultant, Bob Logan, asks the question:

> *What was the difference with these two movements? Why did one movement have great impact long after the death of its founder, John Wesley? Logan believes that Wesley had a reproducible system. Wesley made sure priority was given to train apprentices and raise up leaders to preach, plant churches and lead the hundreds of small groups that began.*[71]

---

[71] From a church growth seminar held in Auckland, NZ, August 1994.

Bill Hybels says:

The local church is the hope of the world, and its future rests primarily in the hands of its leaders.[72]

Author and pastor, Jerry Cook, speaks of Jesus spending a third of His life in public ministry, a third with His Father, and a third with His disciples. Jesus modelled discipleship.

What a fantastic model for us. But the difficult thing is to do it, and that is perhaps because it is not a quick-fix and doesn't have short-term gains. Discipleship is very much a long-term strategy.

Here are some honest questions to ask yourself that will hopefully motivate and activate you towards some life-changing decisions.

- Who are the people you are regularly meeting with who you see as potential leaders?
- Who are you discipling?
- Who are you targeting?
- Who are you mentoring?
- Who are the leaders into whom you are investing your time?

"How can I mentor, coach, or disciple somebody?"

Here are a number of ways:

- I do, you watch.
- I do, you help.
- You do, I help.
- You do, I watch and encourage.

---

[72] Ibid., Hybels, *Courageous Leadership*, p. 27.

The function and effectiveness of new churches and new groups is directly linked to the mentoring and coaching function. Begin to spend time with key people once or twice a month. I usually do this over breakfast or lunch; that's how it works for me. Find a regular time (make sure it's consistent) that works best for you. During our time together, we cover four topics with questions.

1. How do you feel about your **relationship with Christ**? Be very specific with these questions. For example, I may ask, "How is your prayer life right now?" They may reply, "It's OK." Dig deeper. "Do you pray every day? . . . approximately how long?" It's very surprising to discover all was not well when I thought things were healthy.

2. How is your relationship with your **family**?

3. How do you feel it is going in your **ministry areas**? Where are the **pressure points** in your life right now?

4. What are **two questions** that you have? *(Of course, the last two questions could relate to any area of life.)* This question relates to a **specific or major ministry** area, e.g., the leadership of their ministry, etc.

In addition to this, I have used a mentoring grid.[73] I have found it to be a helpful tool that covers personal growth and ministry activity.

Mentoring Grid		
	Personal Growth	*Ministry Activity*
Evaluate		
Plan		
Study		

---

[73] Logan, Robert E. *Eight Keys for Starting and Multiplying Churches*, p. 28. (*The Church Planters Toolkit*, 1994, ChurchSmart resources.)

This grid allows you to get very specific and helps stay focussed.

Some have chosen a book for their discussions. Go with what works for both of you. John C. Maxwell has written some classic works, and I suggest the following.

- *Developing The Leader Within You.*[74]
- *Developing The Leaders Around You.*[75]
- *21 Irrefutable Laws of Leadership,*[76] and
- *Courageous Leadership*[77] by Bill Hybels.

For those who are being mentored, don't see just one person fulfilling every aspect of this mentoring role. There usually are many mentors whose wisdom and inspiration we can draw upon.

We can also be mentored or coached by people we have never met, through podcasts, CDs, DVDs, and other resources via the Internet. This isn't a substitute to meet with people face-to-face to disciple and mentor us. But what a wonderful tool to add to our discipleship toolbox, allowing us to develop personally, and in turn, serve people in more fruitful and healthy ways.

Leaders, it is a priority to disciple and mentor others. In God's word we see an example of this.

- Jethro mentored Moses.
- Moses mentored Joshua.
- Naomi mentored Ruth.
- Ezra mentored Nehemiah.
- Elijah mentored Elisha.
- Jesus mentored the 12 disciples, spending extra time with Peter, James, and John.

---

[74] Second Edition, Thomas Nelson, 2001.
[75] Thomas Nelson, 2005.
[76] Thomas Nelson Publishers, 1998.
[77] Grand Rapids: Zonderman, 2002.

- Barnabas mentored John, Mark, and Paul.
- Paul mentored Timothy, Priscilla, and Aquila.
- Priscilla and Aquila mentored Apollos.

In Exodus 18, we see Jethro, Moses' father-in-law, give him very insightful instruction. He told Moses to continue to represent the people before God. We do this through prayer. Then he instructed:

> *Teach them God's decrees and give them His instructions. Show them how to conduct their lives. Select capable honest men who fear God and hate bribes. Appoint them as leaders over groups of one thousand, one hundred, fifty, and ten.*[78]

Jethro was encouraging Moses to disciple, mentor, and coach people so that he wouldn't wear out himself or the people. Moses then would be able to handle the pressures, and people would go home in peace.[79]

In Acts 6 we see the same thing happening. As the church multiplied, they needed to spend time in prayer and teach the Word of God. Leaders, I would suggest this would have also been one-on-one and face-to-face with people. Another way to say this is discipling. They instructed the believers to select men who were well-respected, full of the Spirit and wisdom, to run an effective feeding programme.[80]

> If you are planting for a year, plant grain. If you are planting for a decade, plant trees. If you are planting for a century, plant people.

> *People who have mentored and discipled others have left a fantastic legacy. John Hurston mentored*

---

[78] Exod. 18:20-21, NLT.
[79] See Exod. 18:17-23.
[80] Acts 6:2-4, NLT.

> *David Yonggi Cho. Paul Kauffman of Asian Outreach mentored David Wong, who in turn is mentoring the new Asian outreach director. From the age of thirteen, painter and sculptor, Michelangelo, was mentored by the painter Ghirlandajo. Leo Tolstoy mentored Boris Pasternak, the author of Doctor Zhivago. Beethoven spent three years under the mentoring of Haydn. Over half of all Nobel Prize winners were once apprenticed by other Nobel winners.[81]*

Ron Lee Davis goes on to say:

> *In many ways, the history of the highest, most enduring achievements of our culture is also a history of the mentoring process.*

Every sports person who is at the top of their game is being mentored and coached by somebody, sometimes multiple coaches: some for diet, another for specific athletic skills, and another for developing the psychological aspect. If this is being done to ensure a win in a sports race, how much more important is the planting of churches and winning people for Christ!

One of the thrills of a mentoree is when he gets to meet a highly respected mentor. This happened for me a number of years ago when I met with David Yonggi Cho in Seoul, Korea. It was a defining moment for me personally—to hear the stories from the man himself that I had only read in books and magazines. When thinking about this meeting, I find myself increasingly fired up and passionate about continuing to pursue the call of God. This is the power of leadership.

We all, to some extent, need to realise that as we mature, we have this influence in people's lives, and we need to use that 'power' carefully, wisely, and positively.

---

[81] Davis, Ron Lee. *Mentoring: The Strategy of the Master.* (Nashville: Thomas Nelson Publishers, 1991), p. 19-20.

An ancient Chinese proverb says:

If you are planting for a year, plant grain. If you are planting for a decade, plant trees. If you are planting for a century, plant people.

One of the main ways in which Jesus transformed the world was by pouring His life into the 12. What an amazing legacy He left!

What legacy will you leave the world?

REFLECTION

The church is the hope of the world, and its future rests in the hands of its leaders.

1. What do you think of Hybels' words?

_____

_____

_____

2. Can you think of any people who were involved in a discipling, mentoring-type relationship with you?

_____

_____

_____

3. Can you think of a person you are presently discipling and preparing for life and leadership?

_____

_____

4. How effective do you think your input and influence in their life is? What are two things you could do to improve this?

_____

_____

_____

8 THE POWER OF VISION

With any list about what a leader is, I still believe vision has to be a major factor, if not the number one element in leadership.

I f the definition of a leader is *to complete a task,* then simply put, leaders want to *do* something, *achieve* something, or *change* something! Why? Because they have a vision, a dream, or a cause which demands it!

Bill Hybels says:

For me, it's said most crisply this way: Vision is a picture of the future that produces passion.[82]

Vision appears to be a key not only in leadership, but also in every individual as well as each church.

- Vision releases us to see as God sees.
- Vision provides strength for every challenge.
- Vision attracts and releases dormant potential.
- Vision turns individuals into a team.

---

[82] Ibid., Hybels, *Courageous Leadership*, p. 32.

- Vision creates passion in us.
- Vision moves me into the future and I see the present as the past.[83]
- Vision empowers me to commit to God's plan.
- Vision keeps the clutter (other things) out of my life.
- Vision enables and empowers me to live carefully.
- Vision enables me to live!

Paul Yonggi Cho makes a very challenging assertion in his work, *The Fourth Dimension.*

> *God has been using this language of the Holy Spirit (i.e., visions and dreams) to change many lives. Look carefully when you read Genesis 13:14-15:*
>
> *The LORD said to Abram, after Lot had separated from him, "Lift your eyes now and look from the place where you are—northward, southward, eastward, and westward; for all the land which you see I give to you and your descendants forever."[84]*
>
> *God did not say, 'Oh, Abraham, I'll give you Canaan. Just claim it.' No, very specifically God told him to stand from his place, look northward, southward, eastward, and westward, and that He would give that land to Abraham and his descendants. Seeing is possessing.[85]*

By the way, for your encouragement, Abraham, never saw the complete fulfillment of his descendants as many as the stars in the sky

---

[83] De Jong, P.

[84] NKJV.

[85] Cho, Dr. Paul Yonggi. *The Fourth Dimension.* (Plainfield: Logo International, 1979), pp. 46-47.

or the sand on the seashore.[86] Abraham saw only *some* of the reality of that promise come to pass; it was later generations that realised it and walked in it. But Abraham saw in another realm! Often the vision that God gives us is beyond us! Other generations walk in what we have seen and prayed for.

Down through history, as long as man has walked with God, certain men and women have stood out. Why? *Their walk with God was consumed with vision.*

Jesus always presented His disciples with a big vision:

Go . . . and make disciples of all the nations . . .[87]

And you will be my witnesses in Jerusalem, and in all Judea and Samaria, and to the ends of the earth.[88]

In other words, the disciples went out and preached the Gospel 'everywhere'. Continuing throughout the book of Acts we see that the disciples did exactly what Jesus had told them to do.

I am convinced churches cannot be planted without vision.

I saw the LORD. He was sitting on a lofty throne, and the train of his robe filled the Temple.

Isaiah 6:1, NLT

Isaiah saw something and it changed his life forever.

In Ezekiel 37:1, the prophet saw something in the midst of a hopeless time in Israel's history that empowered him and others. Elisha saw Heaven's armies protecting them and fighting for them.[89]

The prophet Habakkuk encourages us to go and position ourselves before God and wait to see what He says, then write the

---

[86] See Heb. 11:12.
[87] Matt. 28:19a, NKJV.
[88] Acts 1:8b, NIV.
[89] See 2 Kings 6:13-17.

vision down so we can run with clarity and in a focussed way towards what HE has said.[90] The Apostle John had such a vision . . . simply read the book of Revelation![91] Remember John was in his late 80s or early 90s, exiled on the Island of Patmos simply for preaching God's Word. He was incarcerated with criminals. He had no family, no friends, and no church to attend. Yet on the Lord's Day, he set himself aside and was in the Spirit. He set himself apart and vision came. John didn't wait for the worship leader or musicians, or someone else to create the right atmposphere; He was his own worship leader and carried Heaven's atmosphere wherever he went.

Before we come into a large place in our experience, we need to come into a large place in our spirit.

We see a wonderful lesson here: *For a leader, vision is intentional.* Vision is received, adjusted, and refreshed as the leader sets aside time to meditate, pray, muse, and imagine, allowing God to speak. We can only give what we receive from Heaven.[92]

Hebrews 11 is filled with people with whom God spoke and received a vision. *Did they have vision, and then receive faith to fulfill it, or did they have faith, then God gave them a vision?*

> *They did not receive what was promised, but they **saw** it all from a distance and welcomed it.*

Hebrews 11:13, NLT, emphasis added

They didn't pray the problem, they prayed according to the promise. *What do you see, and what are you welcoming into your life and into your world?*

---

[90] See Hab. 2:1-3.
[91] See Rev. 1:9-11.
[92] See John 3:27, NLT.

If the vision can be fulfilled in your lifetime, I would suggest it's not big enough.

We must remember that vision comes out of the soil of values. These values are the non-negotiables—the things we hold dear, the things we highly treasure. Out of these come godly vision.

For example, we long to see our children succeed in life. Why is this? It is because they are loved and valued; therefore, we long to see them achieve their full potential. Likewise, if the lost are important and valued by us, we will do what we have to in order to see them come to Christ.

To draw on Hybels' earlier statement, we picture their future—our children growing healthy and strong, the lost coming to Christ—and it produces passion and excitement within us.

I would suggest that we only do what we value. How do you measure a value? If we say lost people matter to Christ, and yet we have no strategies, targeted finance, or plans to see them won, I wonder just how important winning the lost is to us?

Some Key Elements of Vision

1. Looking at our own limitations only narrows vision.

Let me say this another way: vision that is of God keeps us looking at Him. It keeps us on our knees. If we are able to fulfill the vision in our own strength using our own resources, abilities, and talents, then the vision is not big enough. *God's vision to each one of us is beyond ourselves.* Only as we link into God, His ability, His power, and His strength are we able to fulfill the vision—not relying on our own strength, but upon His. We all have limitations, but I've discovered limitations are often God's gift to us. Simply allow them to push you towards God and His vision for you.

2. Discouragement comes from the inability to see.

In Psalm 118:5, the psalmist was deeply distressed. However, he saw something that was much greater.

> The LORD answered me and set me in a large place.[93]

As stated before, Elisha's servant saw the Aramaen army besieging them at Dothan, but Elisha saw the armies of Heaven.

> "Don't be afraid," the prophet answered. "Those who are with us are more than those who are with them."

> 2 Kings 6:16

We need to see as the eagle sees—far into the distance. We need to *keep our eyes on God's perspective, not on our own.* Discouragement will rob you of vision. By all means, allow vision to be refined; sometimes it seems that it dies before being finely tuned into what God has desired all along. But never be without vision.

For example, you may have a great desire to plant churches that plant churches. As you pray, that desire only increases. Then you talk to those you respect, and you start to reassess things, and the vision you have seems to lose its glow and slowly slip away. However, sometime later it rises again, slightly different to how you first perceived it, but more in line with God's timing and plan. If vision seems to die, let's not forget that the *death and resurrection idea* is central to Christian thought: *in order to gain our life, we must lose it.* The seed must die before it sprouts new life. So let's not worry if the vision seems to die; this merely allows God to refine the vision that He has birthed in our hearts. It's God's way of allowing us to surrender control in exchange for His control.

Oh the privilege and blessing of a God-partnership. Time is a huge factor. I'm the kind of person who would like things to happen yesterday! Sometimes, days turn into weeks, and weeks turn into years, and years turn into decades. I know this to be true! But I've come to appreciate God's perfect timing in the vision He gives.

---

[93] NASB.

I believe God desires to give each of us a vision. *He has a plan and purpose for each one of us.*[94] Grasp the vision He gives, and determine to hold on to it . . . no matter what may come. *Don't let anyone rob you of that divine purpose He has for you.* Even in the most difficult of circumstances and situations God has encouraged many a person. Why? Quite simply, because they saw God's vision stretched out before them.

Let's understand very clearly that *before we come into a large place in our experience, we need to come into a large place in our spirit.*

3. We need to be careful.

A person who has vision cannot settle for business as usual, even though it leads directly into uncharted territory filled with dangers and risks.

I love the song, "Oceans."[95] We sing so feely and easily—

> You call me out upon the waters,
> The great unknown where feet may fail
> And there I find You in the mystery . . .
> Spirit lead me where my trust is without borders,
> Let me walk upon the waters
> Wherever You would call me.
> Take me deeper than my feet could ever wander
> And my faith will be made stronger . . .

And we wonder why God takes us to places where we have never been before!

When God gives you a vision, your goals, your attitudes, actions, and priorities will change; your whole life will change! Vision demands walking out on the limbs of the branch—that's where the fruit is, but it's also very dangerous. God becomes central in your life,

---

[94] See Jer. 29:11.
[95] "Oceans (Where Feet May Fail)", Hillsong United; copyright 2013.

for you realise that *He must be the centre of it all for the vision to ever begin*, let alone come to pass.

Jesus had an all-consuming, all-encompassing vision that was, and still is, to reach every man, woman, boy, and girl with His Gospel. He is fulfilling this through you and me.

Let's remember that God saved us for two reasons:

1. For Himself.
2. For the world.[96]

I recall hearing the story told of a person who said to Helen Keller once, "It must be terrible to be blind."

Helen Keller answered with these words: "Worse than being blind is to see but have no vision."

Stanley Kubrick's classic film, "Spartacus," tells the story of a revolt against Rome by a large horde of slaves led by the gladiator Spartacus. In the picture's climax, one of the most memorable scenes in cinematic history, the slave army is demolished by the Roman legions led by the power-hungry General Crassus. As Crassus surveys the survivors of the slave army, he has it announced that the penalty of death shall be waived and all survivors will be allowed to live again as slaves on the condition that they give up their leader, Spartacus.

As the slave-General rises to his feet to give himself up, his friend Antonius rises first and cries out, "I'm Spartacus!"

Then the man on Spartacus' left stands and bellows, "I'm Spartacus!"

Then someone at the back yells, "I'm Spartacus!" Before long, the entire company is on its feet, and in an uproar with all of the men condemning themselves to the excruciating death of crucifixion by their unwillingness to give the Romans what they wanted.

---

[96] See 1 Pet. 2:9.

Why did they do this? Why did they give up the chance to live and face a terrible death? The answer is simple: they had been caught up in the vision of a man—the vision that despite the hardships, battles, and frustrations, by following Spartacus, they knew they could truly be free. Humanity's eternal struggle for freedom was what filled Spartacus' vision, and those around him caught that vision until it became their own. His picture of the future produced an infectious passion that gripped the men so much, they were willing to die for it.

In the same way, our God-given vision sustains and energizes us to see its fulfillment.

What is the vision God has given you?

Let's keep our focus on Him and what He has told us to do. If we lose this thrust, this focus, this vision, we move into what some have called the "great omission'. This results in nominalism, loss of vision, frustration in church life, selfishness, and I would suggest, eventual spiritual death.

Let me remind you of a sobering thought: *seeing people come to Christ is the only thing that we will not be able to do in Heaven!*

Let us never lack for vision. Let's reach out to the people that God has placed within our sphere of influence, in our community, in our nation. For those of us who live in the Western world, there are multiple millions who do not know Christ as Lord and Saviour! That's a fairly good place to start, isn't it?

If not us, WHO?

If not now, WHEN?

If not here, WHERE?

REFLECTION

1. "Vision is a picture of the future that produces passion in you." Regarding the future what is it within you that produces a passion, a sense of excitement? Describe it?

_____

_____

_____

_____

2. If you can't think of something, what steps could you take to gain vision for yourself?

_____

_____

_____

_____

3. Have you been focussing on your own limitations? If so, how can you set about changing in this area?

_____

_____

_____

_____

_____

_____

4. "The death/resurrection life idea is central to Christian thought; in order to gain our life, we must lose it." Are there any old ways of thinking or of doing things that need to die before God takes you on into that new thing?

_____

_____

_____

_____

5. If you were to write your life mission in a sentence or two, what would it be?

_____

_____

_____

_____

_____

_____

9 BUILDING OUR BASE

have often found church leaders intensely focussed on building their local church—which is good and right, to a point. However, I believe this can be the product of an unbalanced biblical view. Let me explain.

In Acts 1:4, the disciples were told to wait in Jerusalem until they were filled with the Holy Spirit. Then, of course, they stayed in Jerusalem ministering . . . until they "built their base"? No! They stayed until they were filled with the Holy Spirit, and then moved out—albeit with some circumstantial 'encouragement'.

Jesus exhorted the apostles:

> *But you will receive power when the Holy Spirit comes on you; and you will be my witnesses in Jerusalem, and in all Judea and Samaria, and to the ends of the earth.*

Acts 1:8

In this context, Jesus' desire was that we would be His witnesses throughout the entire world—not just our local community or city.

I have sometimes heard the following statement given as a reason for not being involved in church planting: "We need to build *our* base . . ." Now I want to say from the outset that I agree in the sense that our base (our foundations) must be strong. But often base-building is used as an excuse for not planting new churches in the towns, suburbs, cities, and countries around us. *Some churches have been "base building" for 10, 15, 20 years without any involvement in church planting.*

It is important to be aware that persecution came to the Christians soon after the Feast of Pentecost so they *had* to move away from Jerusalem. We see this persecution at one of its high points, when the Christians "were all scattered throughout the regions of Judea and Samaria." The disciples believed at this time that the command to Go concerned converting only the Jews—their own people. God somehow had to break them out of this mindset.

Persecution caused the believers to flee throughout all of the surrounding regions in Judea and Samaria, and so God's will was achieved as "those who had been scattered preached the word wherever they went."[97]

I pray that God would break us out of the Western world mindset that declares, *self must come first,* or having a 'taking' instead of a 'giving' attitude. Proverbs says:

> *There is one who scatters, yet increases all the more . . .*[98] *And he who waters will himself be watered . . .*[99]

The church that grows has an intentional external vision, not only in words, but also in action. The church that has an internal vision but with no outreach does not grow over the long term. I question whether such a church has a vision at all because *mission is the task of the church as a flame is to fire.* Jesus never told us to build our base to the exclusion of reaching those around us; and 'around' means not only our community, but also the towns, cities, and even countries within

---

[97] See Acts 8:4.
[98] Prov. 11:24, NKJV.
[99] v 25, AMP.

our ability to reach. Didn't Jesus command us to disciple **nations**?[100] By the way, we have more resources now to disciple nations than when this command was first given by Jesus! The first disciples didn't have the ease of travel by cars, planes, push-bikes, or excellent roading networks, the Internet, social media, and many other communication platforms that we have today.

> I pray that God would break us out of the Western-world mindset that declares, self must come first.

Friends, *if we are not actively contributing to the Great Commission in some tangible way, I believe we are not fulfilling the primary function of the church,* which is to "Go into all the world and preach the Gospel."[101] Let's remember, Jesus said, "GO." We often only say, "COME." He says, "GO." We say, "Come." He says, "GO!" I believe it's both. We can host events inviting people to come, but this is always out of a heart to GO!

---

[100] See Matt. 28.
[101] Mark 16:15.

REFLECTION

1. Have you ever seen the 'base-building' mindset? How does this chapter challenge that thinking?

_____

_____

_____

_____

2. If you were to sum up the teaching in this chapter in a single sentence, what would you say?

_____

_____

_____

_____

3. What are the primary reasons for having an outward focus rather than merely 'building your base'?

_____

_____

_____

_____

_____

10 THE PIONEER

In order to discover new lands one must be willing to lose sight of the shore for a very long time.

—Albert Einstein

Now to Him who is able to do exceedingly abundantly above all that we ask or think . . .

—Ephesians 3:20, NKJV

Imagination is more important than knowledge, for imagination takes us to other worlds.

—Albert Einsten

The person who sets out to plant churches that plants churches could be termed a 'pioneer'. Pioneers start something from nothing; they are the initiators. For them, everything is new—new people, new vision, new community.

The greatest risk of all is not to take a risk.

The pioneer is preparing a platform upon which a body of people will work together combining gifts, talents, abilities, and resources to win their community for Christ till He returns.

I am convinced that . . . if we lose our vision for the Great Commission, we then move into remission.

If we lose our vision for winning the lost in our newly planted churches (and in every church), we will lose purpose, direction, and our reason for existing as a church. Disappointment and frustration will result in the newly planted church. In his resource material called, "Growing New Churches on a Shoestring," C. Wayne Zunkel says that there are three types of leaders:

1. Those who can make something out of nothing.

2. Those who can take something and give it structure.

3. Those who can take a structure and maintain it.

Zunkel goes on to say:

> *Most pastors are in category number 3, 'Take a structure and maintain it.'*
>
> *But what is needed for new church development is the first type: People who are able to make something out of nothing. It takes a whole new mindset.*[102]

By the way, discouragement is one of the tools of the enemy to hinder expansion. We will get disappointed, but giving *in* to discouragement, I have found, is a choice.

Building something out of nothing requires a different mindset— a pioneer mindset. Following are excerpts from Ron Simpkins' excellent book, *We Can Take the Land,* where he discusses at length this pioneering mindset in the context of church planting.

> *In history, much time is spent on the era of beginnings. Daniel Boone, Columbus, Magellan, De Soto, Drake,*

---

[102] Charles E. Fuller Institute of Evangelism and Church Growth, USA. "Growing New Churches on a Shoestring," slide presentation by C. Wayne Zunkel, Carl F George.

Joan of Arc, Florence Nightingale, the Pilgrims, and other discoverers fill us with a sense of adventure. We usually see them, however, through the rose-coloured glasses of Walt Disney.

The reality of the pioneer life . . . dealt more with people who had to fight the elements, fever, "savages," and entrenched bureaucracies. It meant lonely nights and the sacrifice of many luxuries. They were not driven by high ideals as much as a compulsion and a personality that didn't seem to fit the world around them. The frontier was less of "Little House on the Prairie", and more of huts made of pieces of sod. Meals were cooked over buffalo chips, and sometimes just bare survival was an effort, but out of it came the greatness of America.

So, too, with God's pioneers. Abraham sacrificed much to found a nation, often giving up palaces to sleep in tents. The prophets seldom fitted the mould of the society they lived in, but their restlessness made them into people whom God could use. Jesus, the pioneer of our faith, left the secure path to take the difficult one.

The pioneer has always been called to a rough, challenging, and dangerous adventure. Greatness is built on the backs of those who break ground. Nameless men and women opened a continent to found the greatest nation on Earth. Benjamin Franklin opened up a world of electricity, Thomas Edison brought us light, Henry Ford broke ground in industry, and the Wright brothers enabled men to walk trails in the sky.

The force of a nation, and of a movement, lies in its pioneers. These pioneers blaze trails that others can follow. The early Church was an explosion that hit a world locked in a rigid mould. Recorded for those three hundred years is the force of a movement, pushing outward at any price. In breaking ground the disciples gave their lives to spread the Gospel across every continent of the known world to reach a lost humanity.

Noah makes the astronauts look tame. He prepared the crudest of boats and went where no man had gone before. He was building this boat-thing for around 100 years. Tell me, how does Noah explain to his friends what he's doing, as there was no water to float anything, let alone what does he say he's building? Then he was going to fill it with animals of every kind. How is Noah going to get them into this thing? Hummmm, yeah right!!

Israel was birthed with a mandate to take the land. When Joshua led the nation out, his life was not in the size of his bank account, but in the fact that they set their feet on land God had promised them. And Jericho's walls did fall! Every revival of divine vision was marked by a warrior-king who took the land was there by God's design. And how powerful today is Israel's restoration as a nation that, once again, is out to claim God's land.

Today in the Kingdom of God, this is still true. Jesus told us to pray, your Kingdom come on earth as it is in Heaven! Jesus spoke of a last-days commission: The Gospel will be taken into all the world, then will the end come (Matt. 24:14).

Paul took the Gospel and planted churches in the eastern Mediterranean for three decades, forging a trail into virgin territory that saw the Gospel spread and the Christian faith grow. The Apostle planted churches in Antioch of Pisidia, Iconium, Lystra, and

Derbe in Galatia during his first missionary journey.[103] On his second missionary journey he planted churches in Macedonia (Philippi, Thessalonica, and Berea) and in Corinth of Achaia (i.e., modern Greece).[104] He likely planted other churches also. He also wrote to, pastored, and visited Christian churches originated by others in Syrian Antioch, Ephesus, Troas, Colossae, and Jerusalem.[105]

The heroes of the faith are the 'Pauls' who break new ground for the sake of Christ and the Gospel.

A romantic vision? I don't think so. It's a call to sacrifice and work.

I have spoken to some of those who are God's pioneers. Their first responses were filled with memories that brought sardonic laughter and stories of hard work and endurance. There was little spoken of the romance that makes fantasies. They spoke of something that, if you survived, it was one of life's major challenges for them. They told me of learning the desperation of prayer. They spoke of the excitement of building a spiritual platform from which God could move in their lives, and in their circumstances, or situations.

> If we lose our vision for the Great Commission, we then move into remission.

After a few jokes about the difficulty of being a "living sacrifice" they often seemed to look far off and tell of lives that have been changed. *They told stories of how they were jerked out of the innocence of the 'womb' of the mother-church and were forced to mature—to become men and women of God.* The life of a pioneer is a great call for

---

[103] See Acts 13-14.
[104] See Acts 16-18.
[105] Simkins, Ron. *We Can Take the Land: A Study in Church Planting,* (Potters Press, 1984).

a person who likes to experience both the good and the difficult life, and see God come through victoriously.

Likewise, New Zealand has been a nation rich with a pioneering heritage. Our history is littered with pioneering men and women. The following are just a few examples of our heroes of faith.

Richard Pearse (1877-1953), "Self-taught inventor, prophetic designer, trail-blazing aviator, and eccentric visionary."[106] Pearse flew eight months before the Wright Brothers made their historic flight at Kitty Hawk in December 1903. In March 1903, Pearse, a "reclusive New Zealand farmer", climbed into a homemade monoplane and flew approximately 140 metres before landing in gorse.

Then there was **Bert Munro (1899-1978)** who set a world

motorcycle land speed record at Bonneville Salt Flats in 1967, riding an Indian motorcycle he had modified. Anthony Hopkins plays Bert Munro in the inspiring 2005 film, "The World's Fastest Indian."

---

[106] Paul Ward, "Richard Pearse: First Flyer"; The New Zealand Edge: article available online at: www.nzedge.com/heroes/pearse.html [accessed 29 May 2008].

Another heroic pioneer is scientist **Ernest Rutherford (1871–1937)**, the Nelson farm boy who split the atom and became the father of modern atomic physics, a 1908 Nobel Prize winner, and one of the greatest scientists of the 20th century.

Kate Shepherd (1847-1934), another phenomenal world leader, and the woman pictured on New Zealand's $10 note. She led

the campaign for women's suffrage in this country. Her work paved the way for a landmark piece of legislation passed on 19 September 1893, making New Zealand the first self-governing country in the world to allow women the right to vote in parliamentary elections. Democratic nations such as Great Britain and the United States did not give women the vote until after the First World War (1918 and 1920 respectively). New Zealand's world leadership in women's suffrage became a central part of our image as a trail blazing 'social laboratory'.[107]

I have also seen this pioneering spirit in the life and work of Christian leaders taking the Gospel into all the world. We have a family in our local church that are strategic leaders in Asia. They are working to establish church-planting movements among unreached people groups. They recently handed their church-planting project over into the hands of national leadership. Through this project, thousands of people have come to know Christ! In another project, they have also

---

[107] 'New Zealand Women and the Vote,' sourced at: nzhistory.net.nz/politics/womens-suffrage, (Ministry for Culture and Heritage), updated 23-Apr-2008.

seen hundreds of churches planted in mega-cities relatively untouched by the Gospel. These are amazing people doing great things for God!

Then, there are **Kalyan and Jessie** and their family who live in Chennai, India. They have been working since 1998 when they started  Harvest Apostolic Ministries, a training and church planting movement in India. As of 2016, 500 churches have been planted. Their dream is that by 2030, there will be 1,000 churches in their network, plus 5,000 more churches through broader Kingdom networking and empowering.

These amazing people are providing pioneering leadership to this cutting-edge movement in the enormous and needy nation of India.

I'm sure as you read this you would have pioneer people scrolling through your mind. The list of these heroes is huge!

New Zealand, as well as most nations, was built upon this pioneering spirit. We must continue to nurture this strength and harness its power and potential for the glory of God and the extension of His kingdom into every nation.

Whatever nation we come from, we must work at taking hold of this pioneering passion to enable us to forge ahead towards new horizons. One never discovers new lands without first leaving the security of the known.

When one is living on the pioneer edge, it's then that one truly starts to live; and in those times of desperation where we reach the end of ourselves, we find the God of 'much more', the 'God of the impossible breakthrough' waiting to do His work in His way. Let's learn to work *with* God, not simply *for* Him. His Holy Spirit is in us for our sake, but comes upon us for others'. What a wonderful partnership.

REFLECTION

1. Do you fit into any of the definitions of Zunkel's three types of leaders? Identify which one(s), and give a brief description.

    1. Those who can make something out of nothing.
    2. Those who can take something and give it structure.
    3. Those who can take a structure and maintain it.

_____

_____

_____

_____

2. Write down your strengths and how they benefit the church.

_____

_____

_____

_____

_____

3. In what ways can you grow?

_____

_____

_____

_____

‖ THE MAIN THING

The main thing is to keep the main thing the main thing.

—Dr. George Sweeting[108]

In this life I believe we can be successful in many things . . . my concern for this generation is that they end up being successful in the wrong things.

—Haddon Robinson[109]

Could it be that we end up being successful in the wrong things? Hear the priority and passion for souls in those who have gone before us.

C.H. Spurgeon. *"The fact is, brethren, we must have conversion work here. We cannot go on as some churches do without converts. We cannot, we will not, we must not, we dare not. Souls must be converted here, and if there be not many born to Christ, may the Lord grant me*

---

[108] Dr. George Sweeting was president of Moody Bible Institute from 1971-1987.

[109] Haddon Robinson speaking to 500 graduates in a seminary in the USA.

to sleep in the tomb and be heard no more. Better indeed for us to die than to live, if souls be not saved."[110]

John Wesley. *"You have nothing to do but to save souls. Therefore spend and be spent in this work. And go not only to those that need you, but to those that need you most. It is not your business to preach so many times, and take care of this or that society; but to save as many souls as you can; to bring as many sinners as you possibly can to repentance."*

Evangelist Reinhardt Bonnke. *"We are to plunder hell to populate heaven for Calvary's sake."*

Paul. *I have had one message for Jews and Greeks alike—the necessity of repenting from sin and turning to God, and of having faith in our Lord Jesus (Acts 20:21, NLT).*

Paul knew exactly why he was on this earth and what his mandate was: the message of repentance and turning to God. He clearly states his life is worth NOTHING to him unless he told others the Good News of Jesus.

> *But my life is worth nothing to me unless I use it for the finishing the work assigned me by the Lord Jesus—the work of telling others the Good News about the wonderful grace of God.*
>
> Acts 20:24, NLT

Paul again states clearly what was the priority of his life and message:

> *I passed on to you what was most important and what had also been passed on to me. Christ died for our sins, just as the Scriptures said. He was buried, and he was raised from the dead on the third day . . .*
>
> 1 Corinthians 15:3-4, NLT

---

[110] Spurgeon planted many churches in and around the London area.

What is most important in your life?

Jesus. He knew clearly what His mandate was. He declared it in the synagogue at the very beginning of His ministry.

> *The Spirit of the LORD is upon me, for he has anointed me to bring Good News to the poor. He has sent me to proclaim that captives will be released, that the blind will see, and the oppressed will be set free, and that the time of the LORD's favor has come.*
>
> Luke 4:18-19, NLT

In the Isaiah 61:1-2 text from which Jesus was reading, there is no full-stop where He ends. It goes on to say in that same verse—

> *And with it, the day of God's anger [vengeance] against their enemies.*[111]

Jesus was clearly declaring that the time of the Lord's favour is now, not the time of God's anger. If that was not clear enough, consider what Jesus says to those people who pleaded for Him to stay:

> *I must preach the Good News of the Kingdom of God in other towns, too, because that is why I was sent.*
>
> Luke 4:43, NLT

In Luke 15, the teachers of the religious law and the Pharisees were complaining bitterly about the fact that sinners and tax collectors were included in the gatherings wherever Jesus was. He was even eating with them! Knowing how the religious struggled with this, Jesus does something He had never done before and never does again. He tells three stories, each one hitting home a bit harder than the previous story: one about sheep, one about money, then a story about a son.

> *There is more joy in heaven over one lost sinner who repents and returns to God than over ninety-nine others who are righteous . . . (v 7, NLT)*

---

[111] NLT.

In the same way, there is more joy in the presence of God's angels when even one sinner repents. (v 10)

We had to celebrate this happy day. For your brother was dead and has come back to life! He was lost, but now he is found! (v 32, NLT)

The master Teacher makes the same point after every story: *"Rejoice . . . celebrate with Me . . . for what was lost is now found!"*

And just to emphasise the same point, Jesus says it again in Luke 19:10:

*For the Son of Man **came** to seek and save those who are lost.*[112]

In Heaven, we will have wonderful, amazing times of praise and worship. The teaching will be inconceivable, new revelation will be—well, wondrous. Connecting with others will be astonishing, and meeting new people will be magnificent, God's presence will be . . . no words can describe it. There will be no sadness or crying, and no funeral directors or health workers will be needed. BUT, there is *one thing* we can only do here on earth: **tell people the Good News and win them to Christ!**

The big question is: *Why are we planting churches? What's the motive?* The primary reason we plant churches that plant churches and new movements is so we can reach more people with the Gospel! That's it. *That's the main thing.*

Pause for a moment and ask yourself: *How is my passion for lost people?*

Church planting must be born out of the biblical mandate:

Go therefore and make disciples of all the nations, baptizing them in the name of the Father and of the Son and of the Holy Spirit, teaching them to observe

---

[112] NLT, emphasis added.

all that I have commanded you; and lo, I am with you always, even to the end of the age.[113]

I know that we keep coming back to this passage, but *Christ's charge is absolutely central to Christianity and to the planting of churches that plant churches.* It's interesting to note that every promise has a condition. This one is no exception: God is with us when we go.

It is very easy for church planters to try to reach those in other churches, but nevertheless, this is a subtle detour which completely misses the 'Great Commission', all while untold multitudes still go into eternity lost. The devil is very, very happy with this strategy and mindset. In many countries, as we have already mentioned previously, millions are without Christ. Nederland in the South, Belgium, France, and Spain, for example, have at least 99% of the population unsaved . . . lost forever! Over 407 million people in Western Europe have no understanding of who God is; they have no personal relationship with Jesus. With this in mind, to go fishing in other churches seems offensive to me.

> There is a crime in the desert more serious than murder; it is to know where the water is and not tell anyone.

We need to be a church that reaches the *lost*. The focus must be clear from the inception of a newly planted church. Before we begin services and as we begin public gatherings, our programming and style must be continually reevaluated. The question we must constantly ask is, *"Are we programming to the lost, or to the dissatisfied Christian?"* I'm not saying that the people from other churches are not welcome. We must minister to them as well, because they are our brothers and sisters in Christ; but they should not be our target group or the main reason we begin the church.

---

[113] Matt. 28:19, 20, NKJV.

The last command[114] must be our first concern; we must reach the lost. Thousands of *people in the Western world* are on their way to a Christless eternity. **The main thing is to keep the main thing the main thing.**[115] *Let's keep off the detours* and *"lift our eyes, and look on the fields, for they are* (already now) *white unto harvest."*[116]

One of the things we cannot do in Heaven is win the lost. We have only a few short years to win people to Christ.

An African proverb says:

> *There is a crime in the desert more serious than murder; it is to know where the water is and not tell anybody.*

We, the church, are the ones who have the living water that will quench the eternal thirst of lost souls in this world, those longing for hope and purpose. Surely, with this knowledge, we must figure out how to win them for Christ. We must do all we can to reach these multitudes. We must seek out those who are lost and dying and share this wonderful free gift with them. What a crime it would be in God's eyes if we merely shared that water among ourselves.

We can't do anything about the harvest of yesterday, but we can affect the harvest of tomorrow.

What will you do?

---

[114] See Matt. 28:19-20.
[115] Dr. George Sweeting declared this phrase at "Amsterdam 86" (Evangelist Billy Graham's conference).
[116] See John 4:35.

REFLECTION

1. Who are the unchurched people in your life? Are you praying for them daily? Write down 2-3 names of those who are open to the Gospel in your world and begin to pray for them.

_____

_____

_____

_____

2. Who are you making regular contact with who don't know Christ?

_____

_____

_____

3. I recommend that you meditate on the Scriptures and quotes in this chapter and allow yourself time to journal what harvest means for you. Let the Word of God read you! What would it mean if these became a living part of you?

_____

_____

_____

_____

12 SOME SAY CHURCH PLANTING DOESN'T WORK!

There is no research or hard data at all to prove that church planting does not work. In fact, the opposite is true.

Every church that is functioning today has been planted! It speaks for itself that church planting works. Imagine if the seven churches spoken about in Revelation (which are in modern-day Turkey) hadn't actively thought beyond their geographical boundaries and planted churches. Would we be here today? Turkey is less than 1% Christian today (some say .05%).

There are many, many factors why some church plants are not successful. But if done well, I'm saying that as an overall biblical strategy, church planting is the best way to fulfill Matthew 28.

Now I understand that some are upset at the ethics involved in some church plants. Simply pulling people out of existing churches and transferring them into a new church does not extend the Kingdom of God. Yet, at the same time, some people do seem to get reactivated and reinvigorated when they move into another church. But let's get real. Pulling people out of one church to enlarge another should never, never be the motive for planting a new church. Biblical Christianity wouldn't even suggest that.

Also, I realise that there are some dysfunctional churches. People are hurt and discouraged, leaders get knocked about, burned out, and their families suffer as well. Some churches do not survive an onslaught of such difficulties, and eventually cease to exist.

And yet the church remains and is still plan A; with God there just is no plan B. The church is filled with people like you and me—imperfect and broken. And yet, when the church functions as God intended, there is nothing on earth like it. Hybels captures this superbly in the following:

> *There is nothing like the local church when it's working right. Its beauty is indescribable, its power is breathtaking, its potential is unlimited. It comforts the grieving and heals the broken in the context of community. It builds bridges to seekers and offers truth to the confused. It provides resources for those in need and opens its arms to the forgotten, the downtrodden, the disillusioned. It breaks the chains of addictions, frees the oppressed, and offers belonging to the marginalized of this world. Whatever the capacity for human suffering, the church has a greater capacity for healing and wholeness.*
>
> *Still to this day, the potential of the local church is almost more than I can grasp. No other organization on earth is like the church. Nothing even comes close.*[117]

Let me expand on this. We have many children who are cared for and receive all the support they need to be strong and healthy. Yet there are many children who are born into very dysfunctional families, abused and neglected, but the children are still there. This does not give us an excuse to abort or abandon them!

The enemy would have us believe that we don't need any more

---

[117] Ibid., Hybels, *Courageous Leadership*, p. 23.

churches. Don't be fooled; it is satan[118] himself who wants to slow us down, even close us down. He hates the church. He is out to steal, kill, and destroy.[119] Let's understand that until Jesus comes, there will always be those churches that are planted with wrong motives. There will be leaders who will cause heartache and those who want to build their kingdom instead of God's.

As Noah may have said as he got out of bed one morning, "This boat sure stinks, but it's the only one afloat." *Remember, the church is the only boat afloat and there is a storm raging outside!* It is God's only plan. These things wouldn't be if we lived in a perfect world, but unfortunately we don't live in a perfect world. *Let's not abort church planting!*

Churches are not perfect (actually, which one is?); but some churches are so unhealthy and what happens within their walls is just downright unacceptable. However, the church is full of imperfect people attempting to live God's way in order to produce an outpost of God's kingdom in this fallen world.

Every church that is functioning today has been planted.

Millions of Westerners do not attend a vibrant evangelical local church. Let's not believe the lie that we cannot do anything to impact the nations. Together we **can** do it.

Let's keep planting church-planting churches . . . different kinds and styles of churches, all sorts of churches: musical churches, family churches, street churches, generational churches, teaching churches, serious churches, churches that meet in a home, small churches, middle-sized churches, large churches, cell churches, Samoan churches, Chinese churches, seeker-friendly churches, noisy churches,

---

[118] Note: the author has intentionally chosen not to capitalise the name of satan.
[119] See John 10:10.

quiet churches, youth churches, middle-aged churches, evangelistic churches, teaching churches, hospital churches, hug-everyone-at-the-door churches, hymns-only churches, only-the-latest-worship-songs-sung-here churches . . . and on and on!

Go on . . . give the devil a hard time! Put his lights out! Plan to be involved in impacting a community by *planting a church-planting church!*

To quote Bill Hybels:

The church is the hope of the world.[120]

Friends, church planting is still the best long-term evangelistic method under Heaven!

---

[120] Ibid., Hybels, *Courageous Leadership*, p. 28.

REFLECTION

1. "Church planting is still the best long-term evangelistic method under Heaven!" How do you feel about this statement?

_____

_____

_____

_____

2. What strengths do you see in planting churches to target a particular area of society, e.g., the Spanish-speaking community, youth, families, those desiring biblical and foundational teaching, etc.?

_____

_____

_____

3. What factors come into play in deciding your target group?

_____

_____

_____

_____

_____

13 THE IMPOSSIBLE, YET POSSIBLE, DREAM

God has a dream:

> *Go . . . make disciples of all the nations, baptising them . . . teach these new disciples to obey all the commands I have given you. . . .*
>
> Matthew 28:19-20, NLT

> *He is patient with you, not wanting anyone to perish, but everyone to come to repentance.*
>
> 2 Peter 3:9

I have a dream for **every local church to have a "strategy" to win their community for Christ, and be involved in planting other churches.**

But to realise the dream with its goals and objectives, strategy needs to be implemented. Please don't be fazed or be put off with the words "goals" and "strategy". Keep reading. This isn't about paperwork, it's about heart; it's about finding out what's in the leader's heart and sharing that with the team and praying it through. Dare to write it down somewhere, even if it's on a serviette in a café!

By strategy, I mean "the chosen means to accomplish a pre-determined goal." When seen in those simple terms, it becomes easy to understand why strategy planning is so much a part of daily life.

Every goal or objective is a statement of faith.

For example, Karen and I asked a family around for a meal one evening. Now for this to happen, there were certain things that needed to be done. The meal needed to be prepared, a time needed to be agreed upon, and the children needed to be considered. Once there was a goal in view, a strategy was necessary in order to make that goal a reality.

Strategy is all-important in seeing goals come to fruition in all areas of life, and church planting is no exception. This must happen in both the new church and the mother church. Every meeting in the new church should have a purpose that fits into the overall goal, so the meetings are not isolated events that happen week after week. If goals are not set and a strategy to achieve those goals is not worked through, discouragement easily sets in. Churches can get so easily involved in many, many things—all good, too—but are they the right things? In fact, we can be successful in many things, but it could be that we end up being successful in the wrong things.

GOALS

It is necessary to have a goal (an objective) in view before we have a strategy. Many churches and individual Christians have strategies but no defined goals or objectives. This can become very frustrating, and often a good idea ends up on the pile of good ideas that we tried once, but then discarded. Why does this happen? Perhaps because there was no purpose or meaning, or more exactly, no goal.

For too long the local church has said, "We are the church, so be committed to it, work in it, work with it, give to it, pray for it. . . ." But many times we have failed to give purpose or meaning to what we do!

As local churches leaders we need to ask: "Why are we here?" Vision and philosophy of ministry answer this question.

The next questions are as important: "**What** are our goals and objectives?" and, "**When?**" Establishing the answer to these questions will be a key to growth.

Then, "**How** should this take place?" Strategy answers this question.

Reviewing the above questions is a highly spiritual exercise and may take much time as well as prayer and fasting to finalize an answer.

Dr. Wagner, in his book, *Strategies for Church Growth,*[121] lists five characteristics of good goals, which I like to recall a little differently (so it helps me to remember!) by using the acronym S.M.A.R.T.

- **Significant**

- **Measurable**

- **Attainable**

- **Relevant**

- **Time-bound**

> **Significant**. The goals you set must have the 'stretch' element in them—significant enough to cry out to God. The goals that are set must be large enough to produce a challenge. In order to gain strength, faith— like physical muscles—must be constantly stretched.

---

[121] Wagner, C. P. *Strategies For Church Growth*, (City Regal Books, 1987), pp. 26, 170-171.

Measurable. You know if you have succeeded in reaching your goal. "Igniting Church Planting Movements" is an example of a mission or vision statement. It's not a measurable goal, however. 'We want to see 20 churches planted by 2025' is a goal. It's measurable.

Attainable. Constantly setting goals that can never be attained is counterproductive. Goals must be significant, but not become pipe dreams. If goals are constantly unattainable, discouragement occurs and trust in leadership begins to erode.

Relevant. Be sure you set the right goal. Research is essential. Goals for the future must be relevant to past performance. This is part of what I mean by 'Attainable'—if it's not really relevant, it will not be attainable.

Time-bound. There must be a definite time frame to it. You then know whether you have failed or succeeded. That's why an insecure person finds it very difficult to set goals. Accountability is also necessary. If you are the one setting the goal, make yourself accountable to someone other than yourself and God.

Ownership of goals is essential. Goals and objectives must become personal. The people involved in accomplishing the goal with you must feel that the goal belongs to them. Two signs of goal ownership are:

- Commitment of money, and
- Commitment of time

Let's remember that **every goal or objective is a statement of faith.**

Looking at growing churches trans-denominationally, it seems that growth happens where it is planned.

We need to ask questions if the goals are not met:

1. It may be the right goal, but is the timing correct?

2. Is the method appropriate in this situation?

3. Are our motives right?

4. Does it need a different leader, or more resources?

In fact, goal setting (or establishing objectives) has been a catalyst and focus for church health in a wide range of churches and movements around the world. Goals give us something to aim for; these objectives help us focus our time and effort, and can aid us in setting the appropriate priorities.

The Australian Assemblies of God Story

I mentioned that I had the privilege of spending some time with one of my heroes, Dr. David Yonggi Cho. It was in 1979 at a church growth conference that Dr. Cho was invited to speak. One of the hosts was Frank Houston, then the leader of the Australian Assemblies of God (AOG) movement. As such, the AOG was heavily represented at this conference. I'd read many of Dr Cho's books, and have been greatly impacted by them.

I remember this particular morning we had a breakfast with him. In our conversation I brought up the Australian Assemblies of God movement. Dr. Cho leaned back in his chair with a mischievous smile and looked into the distance and quietly said, "Oh I remember that. Leaders spoke about how difficult and hard things were. They talked about how they needed more resources, and the churches were small and struggling. It seemed like everything was hard."

I asked, "So, what did you do?"

He said, "**I talked about faith**. I spoke on faith every day. I hit them with faith. Then on the last day I simply asked every lead pastor to write on a piece of paper goals for their churches . . . goals such as, how many people they could believe God for in their church, and how many churches they could plant."

The graph below tells it all.[122] Note that the AOG had been growing, but there was a huge growth curve that began soon after that particular conference. Cho, and the AOG leaders, and people such as, C.P. Wagner, put this down to the simplicity of writing down God-

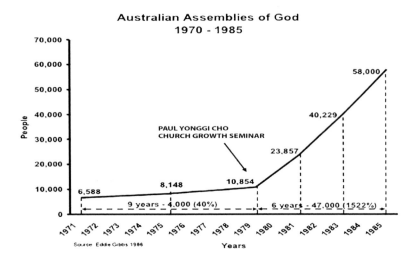

inspired faith goals. It is one powerful example of setting specific faith goals.

It shows that setting goals demands clear definition, releases faith, focusses effort and expenditure, awakens objectivity, and brings accountability. It takes guts to set faith goals, but when a person inspired by God takes the time to hear from Him and sets specific objectives, it's empowering and transformational—life-changing, really.

Strategy

Now let's talk about how to get from here to there; it's called STRATEGY.

---

[122] Ibid., Wagner, *Churchquake,* pp. 149-151.

Strategy is simply the chosen means to accomplish a goal that has been set. You know by this time that God wants you to be involved in a certain area of ministry and so you've set a goal accordingly. To achieve the goal, there needs to be a decisive strategy. We need to plan the steps ahead definitively, and this takes time and effort. It may require more research as well.

It is interesting to note that growing churches, and churches that multiply, have a very clear philosophy of ministry: they know why they are there and they have a clear strategy for winning their community and nation to Christ. Clear objectives and strategy are very intentional. For example, you are waiting at the bus stop for the next bus. The bus comes along; it is full of people. The bus is going somewhere, but it doesn't have a destination on it. Would you get on the bus? It could be the newest bus in town, the people may even seem very happy. However, it's not going anywhere . . . it has no defined destination.

I don't know about you but I would like to know where the bus is going first! I wonder how many people will want to get off the bus after several hours or days of riding because it's travelling aimlessly?

Strategy to meet our goals in all areas of life is certainly a priority, and planting church-planting churches is no exception.

Imagine for a moment if every evangelical church in every nation set goals and formulated strategies. I believe men and women would rise to the forefront where they otherwise would have been content to sit back. Finances would be released in greater measure than ever before, enabling us to disciple the nations for Christ.

Is the dream possible? I am convinced of it!

REFLECTION

1. How important is strategy and goal setting in a task such as planting a church?

_____

_____

_____

_____

2. What does the acronym S.M.A.R.T. stand for?

_____

_____

_____

_____

3. What personal goals do you have for this year? For your life? Write them down and share them with a close friend.

_____

_____

_____

_____

_____

_____

4. What church Multiplication goals do you have for this year? If you don't have any, what would be a good start?

_____

_____

_____

_____

_____

_____

_____

_____

_____

5. What are some church planting goals / objectives for the next 2, 3, 5 years?

_____

_____

_____

_____

_____

_____

_____

_____

14 TWO KEY FACTORS

What are the two key factors that will empower people to keep pioneering and planting church-planting churches? This may also answer, "Why are people hesitant about church planting?"

The two main factors are summed up in two words: sustainability and expectations.

1. Sustainability

In the past we prioritised the church (church plant) over family, finances, and relationships. Not purposely; it was mostly very subtle and unintentional. So how about we church plant another way?

The reality is, if you are in a small town or village, or even a larger city, it may be a church where you, as the lead pastor, will be bi-vocational for many years. In fact, it could be necessary to be bi-vocational for decades. *And that's absolutely fine.* So get a great paying job so you have money and resources for your family, and good breaks away. Make sure bills can be paid on time and you are able to financially bless your family and others.

Don't start programmes, meetings, courses, and ministries out of need. Realise there will always be a need. Start every programme, ministry, or meeting out of strength. Get others on board to lead them. Plant everything out of strength.

For example, if there is no one to run a youth group, don't run one till the right person turns up. Pray a leader in. If you have few musicians and singers, please don't spend one hour singing and grinding through the song list, inflicting out-of-tune or unskilled musicians and singers on people. That's not sustainable, and may I say it's not glorifying to God. If music isn't a strength, use vocal tracks, or hire someone, or use a guitar or a keyboardist and simply sing 1-2 worship songs. You do have options! Don't do things just because another church does them.

What gifts, talents, and treasures has God given to your church? Find them, develop them, and release them.

> **The key factors are sustainability and expectations.**

Instead of majoring on weaknesses, major on what you do well, and build your church on your strengths. If you're going to do something, do it with excellence (excellence is doing the best you can with what you have). Remember, a church plant (or church meeting) is not an isolated event; it's a process in a very long and wonderful journey, and you want that journey to be exciting—a joy, not a drudgery. It may be exciting for or during the first month, but remember you are there for decades.

Steve Addison, in his well-reseached book, *Movements That Change the World,*[123] gives some important examples of sustainable and unsustainable church planting strategies.[124]

---

[123] Addison, Steve. *Movements That Change the World,* (Missional Press, 2009); pp. 112-113.
[124] See APPENDIX E, "Church-Centric or Kingdom-Centric?"

Unsustainable Church Planting Strategies	Sustainable Church Planting Strategies
Fully fund every church plant	Train church planters to raise funds or become tent makers.
Provide a coach for every church planter	Equip established church planters to coach the next wave of church planters
Provide long-term subsidies for struggling church plants	Allow the new church to take responsibility
Parent churches take responsibility for budgeting and administration of church plants	Empower church plants to set up their own systems
Centrally plan and coordinate where and when churches are to be planted	Expect churches to seek God, do the research, and multiply churches wherever there is a need
Start a church	Multiply churches
The denomination solely responsible to identify and recruit church planters	Every church planter trains apprentices on their team for future church plants
Satellite congregations remain completely dependent upon the sending church	Satellite churches quickly graduate to interdependence and become multiplying hubs
A movement held together by tight organizational systems of control	A movement held together by a common cause and relationships

2. Expectations

This is the second key factor. If your expectation is to reach 10% of the town and you have never led a small group or planted a small church, wisdom would suggest your expectations may be dashed. If you are planting a church with the expectation of a full-time income, that's a wrong motive to plant. Expectations again could be dashed. If your expectation is to have 200 people in your church in 2 years and you have never ever led 200 people in your life, expectations could be dashed.

I know of leaders, people, and churches whose expectations weren't met and have moved from disappointment into the cul-de-sac of discouragement. They have never planted a church again, and some dropped out of ministry altogether.

Therefore, make sure your expectations are realistic, allowing for both faith and wisdom, so you do the possible and leave room for the supernatural God-factor of the impossible.

REFLECTION

1. How is the sustainability of what you are doing?

_____

_____

2. Is what you are doing today sustainable in 5-10 years from now?

_____

_____

3. Do you feel your expectations are realistic? Where do your expectations need to be adjusted?

_____

_____

4. How do you feel about Steve Addison's list of unsustainability and sustainability?

_____

_____

_____

_____

_____

_____

15 OIKOS

Our circle of influence—"Oikos: It's God's key to the natural and rapid spread of the Good News!"

—Tom Wolf

The average person has 20-30 people in his or her sphere of influence, with a number of these being non-believers. This is usually not the case with people who have a long history with Christianity as they lose contact with their unchurched friends. Of course, this is only changed as we specifically focus on those who do not know Christ as Lord and Saviour.

The *oikos* concept is a key to evangelism in every local church; it's also a key for the newly planted church. Why? Because the new church is small and people know full well what they are unable to do because of limited resources. This is a proven evangelistic concept that a new church will be able to use straight away.

Oikos is the Greek word[125] meaning, "a household; a house of people."

> *Believe in the Lord Jesus, and you will be saved—you and your **household**.*[126]

Mission Professor, Dr. Tom Wolf, says this about an *oikos*:

> *A social system composed of those related to each other through common ties and tasks. It is God's key to the natural and rapid spread of the Good News.*

Small groups of connected people populate the world. You, too, have people you best relate to within your oikos.

Oikos and the Old Testament

The oikos concept is key to evangelism in every local church.

The Old Testament worldview did not see the family as the nuclear unit as we do in modern times, but as an extended multi-generational group. The New Zealand Maori have a word, *whanau*, which is translated as 'family', but it is bigger than the nuclear unit of the Western family. Some Maori believe that their *whanau* comprises over 200 people! Today the world has evolved beyond family ties to involve a close-knit group, such as a group of classmates or workmates.

The Old Testament pictures the household as including several generations in a family—usually four generations including men, married women, unmarried daughters, slaves, persons without citizenship, and sojourners (i.e., resident foreign workers).

---

[125] Bullinger, E.W. *A Critical Lexicon and Concordance* (Zondervan, 1978), pp. 386-387.
[126] Acts 16:31, emphasis added.

In Genesis 12:3, it says that through Abraham,

All the families of the earth shall be blessed.[127]

When Joshua spoke to the children of Israel prior to their settlement of the land, he intended to inspire them with these words:

> *But if serving the LORD seems undesirable to you, then **choose** for yourselves this day whom you will serve . . . But as for me and my household, we will serve the LORD.*

Joshua 24:15, emphasis added

Joshua urged the people to choose carefully, but his leadership and influence had already determined the course that his *oikos* would take.

Oikos and the New Testament

God continues to focus on households, i.e., friends, extended family, relatives—those with common interest and the same work environment.

In Mark 5:19,[128] Jesus instructed the man he had delivered of demons:

> *Go home to your friends [oikos] and tell them what great things the Lord has done for you, and how He has had compassion on you.*

Jesus knew this man's testimony and influence would powerfully effect the spiritual future of his household and the region.

After Zacchaeus was converted, Jesus announced to him:

> *Today salvation has come to this house [oikos] . . .*

Luke 19:9

---

[127] NKJV. See also Deut. 12:7; 14:26; Josh. 7:14.
[128] NKJV.

When Jesus healed the son of the royal official, "he and all his whole household [oikos] believed."[129]

Peter came to Christ as a result of his brother, Andrew, someone in his oikos.

> *He [Andrew] found first his own brother Simon and said to him, "We have found the Messiah . . ."*
>
> John 1:41, NKJV

Another disciple, Nathaniel, came to Christ as a result of his friend, Philip, who said to him:

> *We have found Him of whom Moses in the law, and also the prophets, wrote—Jesus of Nazareth. . . .*
>
> v 45, NKJV

In Luke 10 we see that Jesus appointed seventy to go in pairs ahead of Him into every city and place where He Himself was intending to visit. Included in the instructions Jesus tells them:

> *Whatever house [oikos] you enter, first say, "Peace to this house [oikos]."*[130]

As I view this verse, plus others in the same passage, I believe Jesus is saying, "Go into all the oikoses'[131] of the world and make disciples."

Verse 6 says:

> *If a son of peace is there [in that household (oikos)], your peace will rest on it . . .*[132]

In other words, look for the person who is receptive to the Gospel

---

[129] John 4:53.

[130] v 5, NKJV.

[131] *Oikos*, plural.

[132] NKJV.

in your oikos (household) which includes your friends, extended family, relatives, those with the same interest, and those in the same work environment, etc. Ralph Neighbour, a Baptist pastor from America who has planted many churches, defines oikos in this way:

> *Those you spend at least one hour every three weeks with . . . most people have 20 to 30 people in their oikos.*[133]

Here is a simple exercise to complete. Write down your oikos group. In that oikos, find out the ones who are *receptive* to the Gospel; there are usually at least two. Just a note here, many people who have been Christians for a long period of time find their oikos is made up completely of Christians. If you are one of these, you need to intentinally find non-Christians to join your oikos. What about the local auto repair shop, hair salon, corner market, other local shops, or joining the Rotary or a sports club? If you have children, link into their oikos through their activities.

Jesus says in Luke 10:7:

> *Stay there [in that house (oikos)] eating and drinking whatever they give you . . . Do not move around from house to house."*

We see an important principle here. When you discover your oikos, don't move from it, but stay in it, and find the people who are receptive to the Gospel.

Friends, it's an exciting concept. *It's a natural bridge to spread the Gospel* and one a new church can use straight away.

Research conducted in 1980 by the Institute of American Church Growth of Pasadena, California, on why people have come to Christ, which shows the oikos concept at work today. Over 30,000 people have been asked the question, "What or who was responsible for your

---

[133] I heard this from Ralph Neighbour during a lecture he gave to the Baptist Union in Auckland, NZ, in the early 1980s.

coming to Christ and your church?" I have done this many times in meetings and the percentages confirm the following chart.

"Who was responsible for you coming to Christ and church?"

1-2%	Special need
0-5%	Evangelistic crusade
2-3%	Walk-in
2-3%	Church programme
4-5%	Sunday school
5-6%	Pastor
1-2%	Visitation
75-90%	Friends or relatives

The facts are clear from the statistics. Most people who are saved don't become Christians through our well-designed programmes or publicised crusades, or even because of the pastor! It's because of *oikos*—the natural networks of friends and family that God has placed us within. It's very simple and uncomplicated.

I agree with Wolf's words that oikos is God's key to the natural and rapid spread of the Good News.

REFLECTION

1. Write down seven people in your *oikos* who don't know Christ as Lord and Saviour.

_____

_____

_____

_____

_____

2. Now choose two who are receptive to the Gospel; determine to be a witness for Jesus to them and commit to praying for their salvation. Find people in your church to join you also.

_____

_____

3. Were you surprised by any of the statistics regarding how people came to be Christians? What were your thoughts?

_____

_____

_____

_____

4. What impact would this knowledge have on evangelism as you and your church understand it?

_____

_____

_____

_____

16 MULTIPLICATION IS IN OUR DNA

I have a conviction that as Christians, we have deep within us a desire and longing to see Multiplication in our lives. It's in our DNA. I also believe, however, that because we have been addicted to addition, we've been held back from His greater purposes being realised in and through us.

For decades, mission leaders have understood that the best way to fulfill the Great Commission is to begin churches with a heart to start new churches. Because they are harvest-focussed, they are birthed already pregnant—ready to plant. These are ones who have a Multiplication Mindset[134] (I call them "MMs"), intentionally planning for exponential disciple-making Kingdom multiplication. A momentum is created with MM churches, whose priorities are focused on empowering more people through discipleship and into Kingdom activities that mature new believers, accelerate growth in the churches, and propagate healthy new ones—a well-established harvest structure.

Jesus has given us a clear and succinct mandate, along with the power and resources needed.

> *Therefore, go and make disciples of all nations, baptizing them in the name of the Father and the Son and the Holy Spirit. Teach these new disciples to obey*

---

[134] See Appendix H: "Having A Multiplication Mindset."

all the commands I have given you . . .

Matthew 28:19-20, NLT

But you will receive power when the Holy Spirit comes on you; and you will be my witnesses, telling people about me everywhere . . .

Acts 1:8a, NLT

Our primary motive and heart behind Multiplication, and all our Kingdom activities, is harvest. Every church established and each new one planted is primarily for this purpose. We are expectant and work to this end: to have a well-established, multiplying, church-planting structure in place that will sustain the future flood of hungry and lost people God brings to us. We are not simply interested in adding numbers to our churches; our desire is to be a commissioning mission station that trains disciples and sends them out.

If we are serious about reaching all nations with the Gospel of Jesus Christ, then we need to begin a virus that is unstoppable— divinely out of control. We will **fish with nets**, not simply a hook and a line; **we'll not just plant a tree, but forests**. We *must* multiply churches, and we *must* network and partner together with other church leaders.

Finally, I leave with you a Scripture that has confronted me, challenged me, disturbed me, inspired me for decades, and kept me persevering for God's best in Multiplication:

Now to him who is able to do immeasurably more than all we ask or imagine, according to his power that is at work within us, to him be glory in the church and in Christ Jesus throughout all generations, for ever and ever! Amen.

Ephesians 3:20-21, NIV

My prayer for you is that Multiplication will mark every Kingdom activity you do . . . for the global harvest, and for the glory of His name. Amen.

APPENDICES

The appendices are simply tools for you to use, all of which I have found extremely helpful in planting churches over the last thirty years.

Remember, we are planting *Christ's* Church, His Bride, His Centrepiece. So let's do everything we can, using every tool available, to ensure the plant is well established, bears good fruit, and the fruit remains!

HOW TO START NEW CHURCHES AND MULTIPLY THEM

Please note, this is a guideline. In some cultures and nations, planting churches can happen rapidly without following this process completely. I simply plead for wise, divine creativity.

When a church is planted it should never be isolated and alone; strength comes from partnering together and networking. With it comes the positive results of accountability within the network.

Let me say that *together we can do the impossible*—we can reach nations, cities, and towns! We bring support, partnership, encouragement, and resource to one another. The outcome are networks and movements, and this is, I believe, God's plan.

We cannot and should not attempt to start and plant churches by ourselves. We need a network of friends to partner with. Together is stronger. Let me push this a little further to say I believe it is unbiblical. But within a network of thriving church plants, your success is much more certain and will be undergirded and strengthened.

How to start churches . . . that start churches . . .

Below are the stages of a new church. There is no timeline associated with each stage. In some countries it's very quick; in other countries it's much, much slower. The key is, go to the next stage only when you have strength in the stage you are in. So then you will be building from strength to strength.

The following are the stages of planting a church that matures and multiplies.

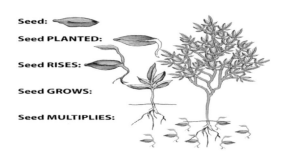

SEED.	This is	continues. . .	continues. . .	continues. . .
Call of God. Strategic Vision takes place. The dream. The DNA is formed.	continually revisited throughout the life of the church.			
Seed PLANTED. Develops as above.	Finalize team Connect groups begin Outreach Prayer Ministry Foundations Marketing	continues. . .	continues. . .	continues. . .
Seed RISES. Develops as above.	continues. . .	Public service Youth children crèche music advertising	continues. . .	continues. . .

Seed GROWS. Develops as above.	continues. . .	continues. . .	Develop new ministries Leadership development Evangelism & assimilation Dynamic services	continues. . .
Seed MULTIPLIES. Develops as above.	continues. . .	continues. . .	continues. . .	Great Commission "eyes". Start new church.

Seed GROWS, and seed MULTIPLIES.[135] The following details this process.

---

[135] The idea is from the "Thomas Stewart Lifecycle," 1986, Fuller Evangelistic Association.

Stage 1: SEED

Strategic Vision

This is where Strategic Vision takes place.

- The tree is already in the SEED. The SEED of a new church begins first and foremost with a vision or dream or idea for a new church. Someone or a group of people must develop a conviction that a certain church must be planted in a certain place, within a people group, or both.

- Spend time in prayer.

- Write down the vision. This will help to clarify the overall objectives to be accomplished.

- It's crucial to clarify the specific target audience or community to be reached.

- If two or more people have this vision, they need to be in agreement about it. Any disunity regarding the vision will not allow the formation of the SEED to occur properly. The seeds of dissension in the beginning of any organisation must be eliminated.

Strategic Planning

- In addition to vision, a new church requires the definition of a clear philosophy of ministry or game plan that describes broadly how the vision will be implemented. An important step in this process is analysing the target group or community. The philosophy of ministry will expand and clarify the vision, describing such things as purpose, priorities, style of worship, and style of ministry.

- Remember to pray when planning and be mindful about being a church that plants churches, so that you plant pregnant.

What does this mean for you? How could this be part of the DNA and culture of your new church?

- Develop your action plan that defines how the church will uniquely reach its target community and why people would want to become involved.

- Remember: fuzzy goals plus fuzzy plans equals fuzzy actions.

Team Development

- The formation of appropriate support systems will aid the church planter in his or her ministry.

- A prayer team and supportive church family are absolutely essential.

- Clarify your accountability relationships.

- Financial support often needs to be arranged. Sometimes additional training is required prior to launching a new church project. Begin sharing the value of tithes and offerings among the team.

- Develop a team of about five to eight people for the new church plant.

SEED Checklist

Simply review this checklist during the SEED stage to determine the items which need to be addressed before moving on to the Seed PLANTED phase. If this isn't done, complications may develop during the PLANTED and / or Seed RISES stage. Remember to only go to the next stage after developing strength in this stage.

- I have developed a clear vision for this new church.

- The initial target audience has been specifically defined.

- I have surveyed / observed my target audience and understand their felt needs.

MULTIPLICATION // INSPIRATION AND TOOLS FOR CHURCH PLANTING

I have formulated a focussed philosophy of ministry which describes the new church's purpose, priorities, style of worship, and ministries.

- Goals and action plans have been decided.

- I have a support team.

- The home church's support and areas of accountability have been discussed and decided.

The Top Priorities For Development

Action Plan	By When	By Whom

Stage 2: Seed PLANTED

For the church, life begins with a seed. In order for a church to embark upon a healthy and effective life, it, too, must accomplish a great deal during the "PLANTED" stage.

Take your time. Once you have started, there is no going back. If a church rushes into its first public worship service without having developed properly, it can suffer the same fate of a miscarried or aborted child. On the other hand, if a church spends too much time in the seed PLANTED development stage, it will lose life-giving momentum and vision.

The key for a successful seed PLANTED stage of a church is to know what needs to be accomplished prior to launching the public worship gatherings. If the essential functions are developed during this time, then birthing a healthy baby can be expected.

Outreach and Evangelism

- Evangelism must be consistent, natural, relevant, and effective. It must have a high value. Remember that's why the church is being planted.

- Understand the needs of the target group.

- Make contact with people who do not regularly attend church; demonstrate genuine Christian love to them.

- Find the evangelistic methods that work best in your community.

- Help new Christians reach their networks.

Group Multiplication

- Start your initial small group / connect group.

- Leaders need to be trained and mobilised to lead small

groups within the new church. These groups are essential for effective evangelism and assimilation, providing a healthy and growing environment for new people.

- Form new groups as quickly as possible. Make sure all new groups have an assistant leader.

- Meet regularly with small group leaders.

- New people are being assimilated into the church through these groups.

- Major ministries, which will start within the following 1-3 years, have been identified.

Ministry Foundations

- Preliminary plans need to be formulated for every major ministry the church will develop within the next 1-3 years. Be flexible. Don't do something because other churches are doing it; build plans out of prayerfulness and obedience to what God is saying to you and your team.

- Make sure everyone is discipling 1-3 people.

- Mobilise your team in preparation for going public.

- Take care of important administration issues.

Seed PLANTED Checklist

- Unbelievers are coming to faith in Christ.

- New leaders are being trained to start connect groups.

- Every small group leader has an apprentice.

- At least two or three groups are in operation now.

- New people are being assimilated into the church through these groups.

- Major ministries, which will start within the next 1-3 years, have been identified.

- Every leader is discipling 1-3 people.

- Perhaps list below five essential ministries that you desire to have operating well within the next 6-12 months, and indicate which of these ministries you have already begun to implement.

The Top Priorities For Development

Action Plan	By When	By Whom

Stage 3: Seed RISES

The new plant begins to RISE above the ground. The birth of a new church is just as exciting as the birth of a new baby. After months of anticipation, preparation, and critical development, that big day arrives when the new church holds its first public worship service. The new church has developed enough of its own strength and maturity that it can confidently and gladly announce to the general public, *"We're here, and we've got something to offer you!"*

Just as the rising of a new plant or the birth of a new baby, the process requires skill and timing, so the initial "entrance" of a new church into the world must be carefully planned and implemented.

Public Gatherings and Worship Services

Often it is important and helpful to have what is often called 'pre-launch' services. This is 4-8 weeks where you run through a full service before the actual advertised public worship services are launched. These trial services allow all the problems to be ironed out and gives everyone a more relaxed atmosphere to learn their responsibilities. This pre-launch period also gives everyone a feel for the meeting venue, the sound system, how it is working for musicians, the children's area, the parking situation, what the needs are for the hosting team, the hospitality and coffee after the service, etc. You can certainly invite people to these 'practice' services.

The following are important to consider in prepartion for your worship services.

- Choose the right time and location. Your first gatherings / worship services make a very important statement about your church. Consequently, you should put a great deal of prayer and thought into them.

- Make worship preparation a special event so that people will truly celebrate God. If you use live music, establish a weekly rehearsal from the start. A well-rehearsed team allows the worship leaders to focus on guiding people into God's presence.

- The critical size needed for effective worship will vary depending on your philosophy of ministry. You'll want to start having services when you have enough people for your style of worship. The facility where you gather should be easy to locate.

- Clearly define your worship style so that it is culturally relevant to your target group. This is particularly important if you plan to attract and assimilate unchurched people into your congregation. An idea is to ask an unchurched friend to critique the meeting, before, during, and after the service. Questions to ask: Are people friendly? Is there in-house speak that you don't understand? What other barriers did you see or find?

- Train your music worship team well. Remember that 30-40% of the service is music. Training cannot be overemphasised.

Children's Programmes

- A major question many parents ask when they consider a new church is, "What does this church have to offer my children?" That question is especially important for those with younger children. Before you start your first service, the question of how you are going to meet the needs of children should be well considered.

- Providing consistent pastoral care for children and their families greatly increases a new church's potential for growth.

- Parents look for three things: 1) a safe and happy learning environment; 2) evidence that their children are cared for and enjoying themselves; 3) proof that they are learning Bible truths.

Seed RISES Checklist

- We have adapted our style of service so that it will be appropriate for people in our target group.

- We have secured an easy-to-find location.

- Our church has enough people to conduct our style of worship.

- Our well-trained music worship team demonstrates excellence.

- We have trained leaders for our children's ministry.

- We provide excellent nursery care.

- Our children's programme is effective in reaching and assimilating new children and their families.

- More leaders are continually being trained. Discipleship is taking place.

The Top Priorities For Development

Action Plan	By When	By Whom

Stage 4: Seed GROWS Towards Maturity

Healthy interdependence and self-sufficiency are key words for this stage of growth. As a tree grows from a small shoot into a midsize tree, then into a full-size tree, its maturity levels are marked by increasing interdependence and self-sufficiency. The tree now stands on its own strength and begins to have an impact on the surrounding community. Likewise, as a church grows to maturity it becomes stronger and increasingly self-sufficient. Essentially, all the growth that occurs in this phase is an amplification of the growth that took place in the SEED and Seed PLANTED stage. The key elements of growth in this phase include the following.

Leadership Development

- In order for the church to experience continued growth, more leaders need to be constantly recruited, trained, and mobilised into ministries for which God has gifted them.

- Use modelling and "on-the-job" training. It's called discipleship. Do all our leaders have apprentices?

- Maintain high organisational standards . . . not perfection, but excellence. Excellence is doing the best with what God has given you.

- Is discipling people part of our culture? (Multiplication will not happen without discipleship.)

- Who is being discipled to plant the next church?

Ministry Development

- The leadership team must guide the process of evaluating, planning, and implementing ministries that accomplish church goals.

- Help believers to discover, develop, and use their God-given gifts in ministry.

- People are being discipled.

Evangelism and Assimilation

- Maintain evangelism as a high priority. Making disciples is a primary mandate for all churches, and requires high emphasis in time, creativity, money, training, and programming.

- Help members to cultivate "redemptive relationships."

- New groups are needed to reach and incorporate new people.

- Implement newcomer orientation. Keep this simple.

- When and where are new churches being planted?

Dynamic Worship

- Focus on active response to God.

- Increase the number of people preparing for worship.

- Keep worship creative and celebrative.

GROWTH Checklist

- Our church is effective in outreach. Are people coming to Christ?

- Newcomers are being assimilated.

- There are at least 6-7 small groups for every 100 people attending.

- New leaders are regularly recruited, trained, and mobilised into new and existing ministries.

- People and leaders are being discipled and are discipling others.

- Our people are mobilised to use their spiritual gifts in ministry.

- Aim for 50-60 roles or tasks for every 100 people attending.

- Ministries are developed according to our philosophy and priorities in order to meet community / church needs.

- Evaluation of all ministries occurs regularly.

- New church plants are being prayed through and planned.

- The quality of Christian character and commitment in our church is increasing. How can you tell?

- Update the 3-5 year plan. Our people clearly understand and are committed to the objectives of our church.

- Our gatherings are meaningful celebrations and help people respond to God.

The Top Priorities For Development

Action Plan	By When	By Whom

Stage 5: Seed MULTIPLIES

Few things in life are more exciting or challenging than becoming a parent. However, becoming a grandparent is also wonderful. Actually, humanity would cease to exist within one or two short generations were it not for the grandparent-grandchild relationship. The reason is simple: We were created to reproduce. Reproduction (multiplication) from one generation to the next is part of our natural job  description as humans and for all living creatures in general. As we have discussed in Chapter 2, we are created to multiply.

The tree grows, develops, and begins to drop seeds, so that new trees are formed. Is the true fruit from an apple tree another apple, or is it another apple tree? I want to suggest it is another apple tree. Let me go further—a church has matured when it has planted another church.

The church is born to multiply. Not only is it a part of the natural job description of the church as a living organism (the Body of Christ), but multiplication is also part of a church's divine job description.

If a church does not multiply, there is something wrong since it fails to do what is supposed to occur by its very nature. Also, if a church does not multiply, its failure could be an act of disobedience to the Lord of the harvest.

The church is born to multiply and will do so if it is healthy. To ensure reproductive health in the church, the following critical elements need to be in operation.

Great Commission "Eyes"

- See the opportunities to reach lost people. A church can multiply if it looks out upon the fields of humanity and see them as ripe for the harvest. This kind of church is committed to reaching the unreached and unchurched people of the world with a view to making them responsible, obedient disciples.

- Embrace church planting right into your church purpose. The philosophy of ministry of a healthy, reproducing church explicitly states that the church *will* multiply itself. If that statement is not present, then the church has not adequately grasped its nature, nor the mandate to make disciples of all nations.[136]

Planting and Implementation

- Establish faith-stretching goals.

- Obtain goal ownership.

- Leadership is needed for new churches. Prayer for workers is the best means to recruit church planters. God loves to answer this prayer!

- Mobilise and supervise church planters. There's that word again—discipleship.

- Help daughter churches start granddaughter churches.

Multiplication Checklist

- Our church is effectively making disciples in its own community.

- Our people are aware that the fields are white, ready to be harvested.

- As a church, we are committed to multiplying other churches in order to make disciples in all nations and people groups.

- Our philosophy of ministry explicitly states our commitment to multiply other churches.

- The church budget demonstrates our commitment to start new congregations locally and around the world.

---

[136] See Matt. 28:18-20.

- Our church has a specific plan to multiply other churches.

- We are implementing our plan to multiply new congregations.

The Top Priorities For Development

Action Plan	By When	By Whom

Remember, these are simply GUIDELINES, not strict rules. It is my prayer that these guidelines are able to work for you as you seek to fulfill the Great Commission that Jesus gave to us.

WHAT IS CHURCH?

I think the West has made church very complicated. I also think that the Western world has complicated Christianity in general. The Bible was never meant for an elite few, nor is it to disseminate information, but is primarily for transformation. We are called to be hearers and doers of the Word. The book of Acts was not called the book of beliefs. It is the book of the *acts of the Holy Spirit* and the *acts of the disciples.*

How would you define church?

Biblically I believe there are three major components that make up church. This does not mean it excludes other references to the Body of Christ or church; it's simply boiling everything down to what Jesus taught what church should be and building on it. I believe Jesus leaves it open, uncluttered, and uncomplicated, for He desires and delights in all sorts of unique and creative expressions of church community. This is what truly empowers Multiplication.

Authority.

① – A group of people who take Responsibility.

1. The Great Command. "Love the Lord your God with all your heart and with all your soul and with all your mind . . . Love your neighbor as yourself" (Matt. 22:37-39).

2. The Great Commission. "Therefore go and make disciples of all nations, baptizing them in the name of the Father and of the Son and of the Holy Spirit, and teaching them to obey everything I have commanded you. And surely I am with you always, to the very end of the age" (Matt. 28:19-20, NIV).

???

3. Two ordinances Jesus gave to us:

- Water Baptism and

- Communion (the Lord's Supper)

Size: How large does a church have to be to qualify as a church? Jesus said, "For where two or three gather . . . there am I with them" (Matt. 18:20). According to Jewish tradition, 10 men (from 13 years and over) had to be present for it to be an official worship gathering. But we see here that Jesus does not genderise or put an age to a gathering of believers, nor does He specifiy where it must be held.

Of course, if the components 1-3 above are valued seriously and adhered to, then it will not stay merely at 2-3 people. As we have already seen, Jesus does want Harvest and Multiplication.

Church can be held regularly in a restaurant, theater, café, church building, school, or home. We are NOT talking about house churches. However, a church is a church wherever it meets. *Let's not define church by where it meets.* Size is usually determined by the leadership capacity and the size of the town. A church is a church as it adheres to the points above.

1. Let's remember the reason WHY we plant churches that plant churches: it is for harvest. The vision is to see people come to Christ and be built into a community of faith and multiply.

2. It is important to have values: Values develop culture. The non-negotiables, or the treasures, are so important.

As an example, the VALUES (or the 5 heartbeats) of Vision Churches International are listed below. They are 5 key core values that we are not prepared to live without because they define who we are.[137]

---

[137] A detailed explanation of these values are on our website, www.visionchurches.com.

Supernatural

Multiplication

Apostolic Leadership

Reaching the Lost

Training Development and Discipling

- Worsup
- WoRP.   Revelation
- Communaty - Famine
          "us + we."
- Mission. Matt 16
          22
          23

WHY PLANT CHURCHES?
. . . MORE REASONS[138]

1. **It is the biblical pattern.** The Book of Acts documents the Holy Spirit's strategy for the spontaneous expansion of the church: Everywhere the Apostle Paul won people to Christ, he gathered them into committed communities—into local fellowships of baptised believers.

2. **Planting churches lays the foundation for discipling whole nations.** Through the presence, proclamation, and perspectives of new people who have come to Christ, every sphere of society feels the impact of Christ's Lordship. Islamic, Buddhist, Hindu, and Confusian societies will not be transformed without social salt, prophetic light, and the ethical fragrance of God's people.

3. **Church planting is how unreached cities, nations, and peoples will be reached with the Gospel.** This includes Western nations. As individual churches multiply themselves throughout a society, a movement surges. Floyd McClung, Jr., is right: "The speed in which churches are multiplied is the only way to measure progress towards the completion of the Great Commission."

4. **We plant churches to reach all levels of society.** Society is a spectrum, a mosaic of peoples. The living links of society are the networks of *oikos* groups, circles of influence composed of

---

[138] New Vision NZ 11, by editor, Bruce Patrick.

family, neighbours, co-workers, and friends. When a church is planted in the various segments of society, the natural contacts of family and community channel the spiritual harvest. Thus, small groups of dedicated people make a disproportionate impact on a broad scope of society.

5. **Churches are planted because it preserves the fruit of our evangelism.** Babies are born into families. New converts should be nurtured in congregations. As new segments of society are reached and the Gospel goes further, new churches are a natural spiritual result.

6. **They are a vital place of nurture for multiple generations of believers.** Many para-church ministries concentrate on certain slices of society, e.g., youth, or a particular social group. When churches are planted, all generations in that particular geographical area can be reached.

7. **It fulfills the responsibility to grow in evangelistic and missionary maturity.** The lost must be won. The nations must hear the Gospel. New lessons are learned, new challenges are confronted, and new territories of the dark kingdom are taken as individuals and groups are won to Christ, and His Kingdom is extended.

8. **It builds into the next generation of congregations the vision for church planting.** What we have received, we freely give. The Gospel has come to us. We must give the same to others: Christ *in* us, the hope of glory. The grace poured into our hearts must never be hoarded. The vision must multiply to the ends of the earth.

9. **It is the channel to the nations for church-planting evangelists, pastors, and missionaries.** God, through the intense prayers of His people, is thrusting out labourers into His global harvest. If we are not a channel for His heart passion to save the lost, He will bypass us and raise up others,

and we will wither and die spiritually. Look around at other churches, which are poignant examples of this truth.

10. **Church planting trains church planters.** We give what we have. We learn as we do. And a new generation of church planters will be trained as we plant churches, forging to the ends of the earth.

11. **Church planting develops new leadership.** Studies have confirmed the fact that the most important variable for the growth and expansion of the local church is leadership. New churches open wide the doors of leadership and ministry challenges, and the entire Body of Christ subsequently benefits.

12. **Church planting stimulates existing churches.** Some are reluctant to start a new church for fear of harming any churches that may already be located in the target community. A new church in the community tends to raise the general level of interest in Christianity. If handled properly this can benefit existing churches. That which blesses the Kingdom of God as a whole also blesses the churches that are truly part of the Kingdom.

13. **New churches grow better than older churches.** Built into new churches is a potential for growth that older churches seem to lose. This does not mean that older churches cannot grow; they often do. Nor does it mean that all new churches grow. Many times they do not. However, growth is more likely in newer churches.

Phil Jones, a researcher for the Southern Baptist Home Missions Board, reports, "If baptism rates per hundred members are used as a measure of efficiency for a church, then young churches are more efficient than older churches. The older the church gets, the less efficient it is in baptising new converts."

14. **New churches provide more options for the unchurched.** Unbelievers come in such variety that a correspondingly wide variety of church options is needed to win them. Fortunately, no two churches are alike, and new churches are different from others even within the same denomination.

Some church planters have an aversion to starting new churches of the same denomination in geographical proximity to each other. This aversion may be wise in small rural town settings, but makes little sense in most of today's urban areas.

In the same neighbourhood one often finds a considerable variety of ethnic groups, social classes, and other social networks, each of which requires a different kind of church. Church leaders who think that geographical location is more important than social networks to the average unchurched person are living far from reality.

I love what Tim Keller has to say:

We want to continually renew the whole body of Christ.

It is a great mistake to think that we have to choose *between* church planting and church renewal. Strange as it may seem, the planting of new churches in a city is one of the very best ways to revitalize many older churches in the vicinity and renew the whole Body of Christ. Why?

1. First, the new churches bring new ideas to the whole Body. There is plenty of resistance to the idea that we need to plant new churches to reach the constant stream of 'new' groups and generations and residents. Many congregations insist that all available resources should be used to find ways of helping existing churches reach them. However, there is no better way to teach older congregations about new skills and methods for reaching new people groups than by planting new churches. It is the new churches that will have freedom to be innovative, they become the 'Research and Development' department for the whole Body in the city. Often the older congregations were too timid to try a particular approach or were absolutely sure it 'would not work here'. But when the new church in town succeeds wildly with some new method, the other churches eventually take notice and get the courage to try it themselves.

2. Secondly, new churches are one of the best ways to surface creative, strong leaders for the whole Body. In older congregations, leaders emphasize tradition, tenure, routine, and kinship ties. New congregations, on the other hand, attract a higher percentage of venturesome people who value creativity, risk, innovation, and future orientation. Many of these men and women would never be attracted or compelled into significant ministry apart from the appearance of these new bodies. Often older churches 'box out' many people with strong leadership skills who cannot work in more traditional settings. New churches thus attract and harness many people in the city whose gifts would otherwise not be utilized in the work of the Body. These new leaders eventually benefit the Body in the whole city.

3. Thirdly, the new churches challenge other churches to self-examination. The "success" of new churches often challenges older congregations in general to evaluate themselves in substantial ways. Sometimes it is only in contrast with a new church that older churches can finally define their *own* vision, specialties, and identity. Often the growth of the new congregation gives the older churches hope that 'it can be done', and may even bring about humility and repentance for defeatist and pessimistic attitudes. Sometimes, new congregations can partner with older churches to mount ministries that neither could do by themselves.

4. Fourthly, the new church may be an 'evangelistic feeder' for a whole community. The new church often produces many converts who end up an older church. Sometimes the new church is very exciting and outward facing but is also very unstable or immature in its leadership. Thus some converts cannot stand the tumultuous changes that regularly come through the new church and they move to an existing church. Sometimes the new church reaches a person for Christ, but the new convert quickly discovers that he or she does not 'fit' the socio-economic make up of the new congregation, and gravitates to an established congregation where the customs and culture feel more familiar. Ordinarily, the new churches of a city produce new people not only for themselves, but for the older bodies as well.

Summary: Vigorous church planting is one of the best ways to *renew* the existing churches of a city, as well as the best single way to *grow* the whole Body of Christ in a city.

These are reasons why it is good for the existing churches of the region to initiate or at least support the planting of churches in a given area.

PROFILE OF A CHURCH PLANTER

This is a common question and I am reluctantly going to give a list.[139] I say reluctantly, because I find God always surprises me with people who I think wouldn't be able to plant a church. Also we often expect the person who plants a church will continue to grow it numerically. Often that isn't the gifting of a pure pioneer church planter. Pioneer planters can take a church from 0-120. (I know this is a wide range, but this also depends on which nation you are in. For example, European nations differ from Asian nations, or the USA, etc.) At these stages other factors need to kick in, such as administrative systems and management procedures. Some people are skilled at these, but some are simply not wired up that way and can become frustrated, and even discouraged. Of course, a team member can assist in these areas, but frustration can, nevertheless, still be the result for the leader. That's okay! It does not mean the end or that the person is unable to multiply.

For example, if they are good people gatherers, very pastoral, and have a teaching gift, yet don't have the skills to manage staff or multiple ministries, and are low in putting healthy systems in place that will facilitate growth, link them in with an apostolic-type ministry and plant another church of 30-50 people, all the while discipling a new person to take the lead.

So with this is mind, here is my list:

---

[139] This paper was written by Tim Keller, Redeemer Presbyterian Church, Feb 2002; the full version is on visionchurches.com.

Firstly, key factors that a planter can't do without. The question to ask after each of these qualities is: *Where have I seen this functioning in my ministry? How and when have these been tested in my life? Give practical examples.*

1. **A clear sense of God's call.** Church planting is not easy. The call of God constrains us to plant. A wise Christian leader has said, "If you can do anything else, then do that instead." They need to be serving with consistency in a church before there is any thought of them church planting. It goes without saying they need to be in a close relationship with God, and have developed healthy habits of prayer, reading the Word, fasting, and giving.[140]

2. **A self-starter.** Is able to take initiative; a pioneer. They are able to start from nothing and make it something for God's glory.

3. **Has a high level of faith.** They have the belief that God is able to do this no matter what. They understand, as much as one is able, it is the supernatural God at work. They are able to dream dreams and see impossibilities become possible. They believe that God will make a way where there is no way. The planter must able to see past the present situation and see the future.

4. **Perseverance is a key factor.** Tenacity is another word. They are able to persevere through difficult and unfavorable situations. As Winston Churchill once said, "Never, never, never, never, never give up."

5. **The planter needs to be able to gather people!** They love people and are able to relate to the lost as well as the found. A church planter is a 'well-liked' person that draws people in.

---

[140] Matt. 6:1-18.

6. **They are able to disciple people and train them.** The question is, do people follow you? A key priority for church planters (leaders) is to disciple, train, and release people for the marketplace as well as ministry.[141]

7. **A supportive spouse and family.** Is your family on the same page, and do they have the same dream as you? Sustainability long-term won't happen without this in place.

Rate yourself on the 7 key factors above (1 = low and 10 = high). If you end up with 35 or less, you really need to rethink leading a church plant. Ask a friend or family member to rate you as well.

So that's my key list!

Here is my secondary list: (I say secondary list as I believe these can be learned and are not essential for a person to plant a church.)

1. *They are able to endure loneliness.* How do you handle discouragements? Often the leaders don't get a lot of encouragement. It can feel a little lonely as you begin with nothing. The price tag of vision is frustration and disappointment. Learn to handle these well. Don't let disappointment lead to discouragement!

2. *Ability to be flexible.* They are adaptable and pragmatic. If it's not working, change it. The church planter needs to be happy with being bi-vocational and at times live within tight budgets, with less benefits than an established church enjoys.

3. *Communication.* Vision, strategy, ideas, events, mission, passion, encouragement, preaching, and teaching, all take someone communicating! *Let me remind you that you cannot*

---

[141] See Exod. 18:17-23, esp. vs 20-21; also Acts 6:1-7.

replace the face-to-face communicator who has a passion from God. Emails, texts, Twitter, and Facebook, etc., are all secondary forms of communication, and in some instances, they are simply bad communication tools. Communication is a continual challenge in this age of multiple and advanced forms of communications. Understand you have God with you, the most creative and passionate communicator ever. Communication skills *can* be learned. Allow God to develop this skill.[142]

4. ***Good management of time, volunteers, budgets, and the myriad of other administrative tasks.*** Job descriptions, the legal, property, and health and safety requirements are huge now. Make sure they serve you, not the other way around. There are *so* many distractions that take us away from His mission.[143] The main thing is to keep the main thing the main thing!

---

[142] See 1 Pet. 4:11a.

[143] Churchplanterprofiles.com is another website with helpful tools to assess your church planting ability, etc.

CHURCH-CENTRIC OR KINGDOM-CENTRIC?

Ian Green challenged us at CpS (Church-planting School[144]) about having a Kingdom-mindset as opposed to a church-centric mindset.

A Kingdom-mindset is the way of Jesus.

Please understand this comes from a passion for the local church. Make no mistake, Jesus is building His church and coming back for His church; He loves His church so much He died for it. I love the church! I've been involved with His church for over 50 years and I'm still passionate about His church. Yet Kingdom is what Jesus speaks most about. The Kingdom is mentioned over 80 times and Jesus talked about the church twice. And one of those times, He says He will build it!

Jesus talked about giving us the keys of the Kingdom. So what keys has God given you for your community? If your church disappeared this week, would people in your city or community miss it being there?

> *My desire is that the yeast of the Kingdom is planted*
> *in the dough of society. We want to bleed Kingdom,*
> *Monday to Friday!*
>
> —Ian Green

Didn't Jesus teach us to pray, "Your Kingdom come . . . on earth as it is in Heaven?" That's not for the future only; it's for NOW!

---

[144] Church Planting School, 2014, Hamilton, NZ.

So let's look at being Kingdom-centric which also breeds and breathes a culture of Mission and Multiplication.[145]

I have categorized them into parts.

PART 1: The Church Plant Beginning Focus *(which, by the way, continues throughout the lifetime of the church).*

PART 2: Leadership and Finances of a new and growing church.

PART 3: Structure of a new and growing church.

---

[145] Note: I am drawing on notes from Ian Green. Also from Tom Wolf and Carol Davis, International Urban Institute. I've also added to the list.

PART 1: The Church Plant Beginning Focus

Church-Centric versus Kingdom- (Mission / Multiplication) Centric

Church-Centric	Kingdom- (Mission / Multiplication) Centric
Individual salvation	Whole household, group salvations
Believers' turf	Unbelievers' turf
From events	To process. The road to salvation is a journey.
Scripture taught for information.	Scripture taught for application.
Fund Christians.	Fund people of peace (Lk 10:1-9).
Begin in facilities.	Begin wherever people are (homes, cafés, factories, offices, etc.).
Celebration – large group.	Cell – small group.
Do ministry for them.	Enable and empower everyone to do ministry.
Build programs and buildings.	Build leaders.
"Our" church.	"Your" church.
Being known by God, His love, His favor.	Being known in hell. The devil shudders as you display Christ, His grace and power.

The Kingdom-centric church is impregnating—or seeding—Christ into society.

PART 2: Leadership and Finances of a new and growing church

Leadership

Church-Centric	Kingdom-Centric
Pastor or lone church planter	Apostolic team
Imported professional clergy	Indigenous convert, emerging leader
Leadership . . . only members	Equipper of emerging leaders
From pastoring a congregation . . .	To pastoring a city
From preaching . . .	To ministry

Finances

Church-Centric	Kingdom-Centric
Funded church planter	Bi-vocational church planter
Heavy financial investment	Minimal financial investment
Church resources for the Harvest	Resources are *in* the Harvest

PART 3: Structure of a new and growing church

Church-Centric	Kingdom-Centric
Needs of the church	Needs of the community—gifted (lay) leaders
Clergy-centered / driven / dependent	Centered and dependent
Body of Christ only	Army of God . . . also
Bound by facilities.	Unlimited. Beyond facilities.
Sunday-only church	Seven-day-a-week church-plant pregnant
Make a disciple	Disciple nations
A well for the congregation—"I'm blessed" attitude	A tree of life to transform a community or city

These are powerful points to examine and take into account. Some of these values should be in the beginning phase, and of course permeate and remain throughout the life of the church.

TEN UNIVERSAL ELEMENTS

After surveying Church Planting Movements around the world, we found at least ten elements present in every one of them.[146] While it may be possible to have a Church Planting Movement without them, we have yet to see this occur. Any missionary intent on seeing a Church Planting Movement should consider these ten elements.

1. Prayer

Prayer has been fundamental to every Church Planting Movement we have observed. Prayer typically provides the first pillar in a strategy coordinator's master plan for reaching his or her people group. However, it is the *vitality* of prayer in the missionary's personal life that leads to its imitation in the life of the new church and its leaders. By revealing from the beginning the source of his power in prayer, the missionary effectively gives away the greatest resource he brings to the assignment. This sharing of the power source is critical to the transfer of vision and momentum from the missionary to the new local Christian leadership.

2. Abundant Gospel Sowing

We have yet to see a Church Planting Movement emerge where evangelism is rare or absent. Every Church Planting Movement is accompanied by abundant sowing of the Gospel. The law of the harvest applies well: "If you sow abundantly you will also reap abundantly." In Church Planting Movements, hundreds and even thousands of

---

[146] Garrison, David. *Church Planting Movements* (ch 3). (Published 1999), office of Overseas Operations International Mission Board of the Southern Baptist Convention, Richmond, VA.

individuals are hearing the claims that Jesus Christ has on their lives. This sowing often relies heavily upon mass media evangelism, but it always includes personal evangelism with vivid testimonies to the life-changing power of the Gospel.

The converse to the law of the harvest is also true. Wherever governments or societal forces have managed to intimidate and stifle Christian witness, Church Planting Movements have been effectively eliminated.[147]

3. Intentional Church Planting

In every Church Planting Movement, someone implemented a strategy of deliberate church planting before the movement got under way. There are several instances in which all the contextual elements were in place, but the missionaries lacked either the skill or the vision to lead a Church Planting Movement. However, once this ingredient was added to the mix, the results were remarkable.

Churches don't just happen. There is evidence around the world of many thousands coming to Christ through a variety of means without the resulting development of multiple churches. In these situations, an intentional church-planting strategy might transform these evangelistic awakenings into full-blown Church Planting Movements.

4. Scriptural Authority

Even among nonliterate people groups, the Bible has been the guiding source for doctrine, church policy and life itself. While Church Planting Movements have occurred among peoples without the Bible translated into their own language, the majority had the Bible either orally or in written form in their heart language. In every instance, Scripture provided the rudder for the church's life, and its authority was unquestioned.

---

[147] Note: I'd like to add that I have seen examples of this is in Western Europe, although China and some areas of Indonesia would contradict this last paragraph.

5. Local Leadership

Missionaries involved in Church Planting Movements often speak of the self-discipline required to mentor church planters rather than do the job of church planting themselves. Once a missionary has established his identity as the primary church planter or pastor, it's difficult for him ever to assume a backseat profile again. This is not to say that missionaries have no role in church planting. On the contrary, local church planters receive their best training by watching how the missionary models participative Bible studies with non-Christian seekers. Walking alongside local church planters is the first step in cultivating and establishing local leadership.

6. Lay Leadership

Church Planting Movements are driven by lay leaders. These lay leaders are typically bi-vocational and come from the general profile of the people group being reached. In other words, if the people group is primarily nonliterate, then the leadership shares this characteristic. If the people are primarily fishermen, so too are their lay leaders. As the movement unfolds, paid clergy often emerge. However, the majority—and growth edge of the movement—continue to be led by lay or bi-vocational leaders.

This reliance upon lay leadership ensures the largest possible pool of potential church planters and cell church leaders. Dependence upon seminary-trained—or in nonliterate societies, even educated— pastoral leaders means that the work will always face a leadership deficit.

7. Cell or House Churches

Church buildings do appear in Church Planting Movements. However, the vast majority of the churches continue to be small, reproducible cell churches of 10-30 members meeting in homes or storefronts.

There is a distinction between cell churches and house churches.

Cell churches are linked to one another in some type of structured network. Often this network is linked to a larger, single church identity. The Full Gospel Central Church in Seoul, South Korea, is perhaps the most famous example of the cell-church model with more than 50,000 individual cells.

House churches may look the same as cell churches, but they generally are not organized under a single authority or hierarchy of authorities. As autonomous units, house churches may lack the unifying structure of cell churches, but they are typically more dynamic. Each has its advantages. Cell groups are easier to shape and guide toward doctrinal conformity, while house churches are less vulnerable to suppression by a hostile government. Both types of churches are common in Church Planting Movements, often appearing in the same movement.

8. Churches Planting Churches

In most Church Planting Movements, the first churches were planted by missionaries or by missionary-trained church planters. At some point, however, as the movements entered an exponential phase of reproduction, the churches themselves began planting new churches. In order for this to occur, church members have to believe that reproduction is natural and that no external aids are needed to start a new church. In Church Planting Movements, nothing deters the local believers from winning the lost and planting new cell churches themselves.

9. Rapid Reproduction

Some have challenged the necessity of rapid reproduction for the life of the Church Planting Movement, but no one has questioned its evidence in *every* CPM. Most church planters involved in these movements contend that rapid reproduction is vital to the movement itself. They report that when reproduction rates slow down, the Church Planting Movement falters. Rapid reproduction communicates the urgency and importance of coming to faith in Christ. When rapid reproduction is taking place, you can be assured that the churches are unencumbered by nonessential elements and the laity are fully empowered to participate in this work of God.

10. Healthy Churches

Church growth experts have written extensively in recent years about the marks of a church. Most agree that healthy churches should carry out the following five purposes: 1) worship, 2) evangelistic and missionary outreach, 3) education and discipleship, 4) ministry and 5) fellowship. In each of the Church Planting Movements we studied, these five core functions were evident.

A number of church planters have pointed out that when these five health indicators are strong, the church can't help but grow. More could be said about each of these healthy church indicators, but the most significant one, from a missionary vantage point, is the church's missionary outreach. This impulse within these Church Planting Movement-oriented churches is extending the Gospel into remote people groups and overcoming barriers that have long resisted Western missionary efforts.

The Value and Power of Networks

(Following is an excellent biblical explanation on the value and power of networks. This was presented by Pastor Steve Graham at a 2011, VCI Retreat, New Zealand.)

"Relationships . . . help the pieces of the puzzle come together." I wonder what you think when you read that? I suspect that for many of us we think that it is saying that if we take the time to connect with other leaders then the pieces of the puzzle of our ministry or of our church will begin to come together. I want to suggest that there is a much deeper way to understand that sentence: that as we connect we realise we are one part of "the puzzle", that "the puzzle" is not my ministry or my church, but "the puzzle" is actually the network of churches . . . and things begin to make sense because I find a place to fit within a network of churches.

I want to show this from three aspects of the letters of Paul in the New Testament. I want to look at the little bits that we often skim, but when we look at them together, we get a picture of how the early church functioned. A picture that is incredibly energizing and will blow our minds about how strongly they thought in terms of a network of churches and how radically they lived that out in practical ways.

First, I want to look at the beginning of the letters, where we meet Paul and his co-writers.

Secondly, I want to look at the end of the letters where Paul greets individuals and we meet Paul and his co-workers. As I said, normally we skip over these introductions and endings to get to the theology in the middle of the letters, but taken together, they have quite an impact and give us a picture of the life of the early church.

Finally, I want to show how New Testament scholars view the early church and summarize this picture that emerges.

The "big idea" is that the early church was highly networked.

The first question then, is, "What does this say about how we think about our ministries and our churches and being part of a network of churches?" And *second,* "What practical steps do we need to take to see networks of churches develop and move forward into new dimensions?"

Paul and his co-writers: We often talk about Paul and his letters. We see Paul as a great apostle and know he wrote thirteen letters. However, consider the following:

1 Corinthians 1:1:

> *Paul, called to be an apostle of Christ Jesus by the will of God, and our brother Sosthenes.*

2 Corinthians 1:1:

> *Paul, an apostle of Christ Jesus by the will of God, and Timothy our brother . . .*

Philippians 1:1:

> *Paul and Timothy, servants of Christ Jesus . . .*

Colossians 1:1:

> *Paul, an apostle of Christ Jesus by the will of God, and Timothy our brother.*

1 Thessalonians 1:1:

> *Paul, Silas and Timothy . . .*

2 Thessalonians 1:1:

Paul, Silas and Timothy . . .

Philemon 1:1:

Paul, a prisoner of Christ Jesus, and Timothy our brother . . .

Yes, Paul wrote 13 letters. However, seven of those thirteen— more than half—have co-writers. If you then,consider that three of the other letters, the Pastoral Epistles (1 and 2 Timothy and Titus), involve Paul writing directly to a co-worker, then that leaves only three letters where Paul writes to a church by himself: Romans, Galatians, and Ephesians. Then I think it is possible to see reasons why each of these were actually the *exceptions* to his normal practice of co-authors, e.g., Romans was written to introduce Paul to the church in Rome in preparation for his visit and to state his understanding of the Gospel. Galatians is a specific defense of Paul's apostleship, and Ephesians is something of a generic circular letter.

I believe Paul was deliberately modelling something by this co-authoring of letters. Paul presented ministry not as the great individual, but as a team. This is very countercultural for us Westerners who have been raised on the model of the great heroic individual leader, the John Wayne-kind of figure who does not need anyone, and boldly leads as a loner. This was theologically important for Paul. We have a Trinitarian foundation to our faith. The trinity says, ultimate reality is relational; it is community. Paul modelled this in ministry and he took the trouble to model it in his letters. Ministry was done in relationship and in partnership with others—in a network of ministries.

Secondly, let's look at the little bits normally at the ends of the letters where Paul often greets people and mentions them by name, often his co-workers. Estimates vary, but scholars identify 81-95 co-workers of Paul in the New Testament, depending on how "co-worker" is defined. If we just stick to individuals who Paul names in his letters, there are 36.[148] These are names we may have heard of—people like Andronicus, Apollos, Aquila and Priscilla, Barnabas, Epaphroditus, Junia, Luke, Mark, Onesimus, Silas, Timothy, and Titus.

Let's look at some of these little bits at the end of the letters.

Romans

Look at Romans 16. Paul is writing to a church he has never visited. He greets 28 individuals, 26 by name (and a mother and a sister of someone named). That is incredible! I have been to Eastside Church a number of times and I could not greet 26 people there by name! And this is in a time and culture without fast and cheap airfares; without Skype, email, conferences at hotels, etc. How did he know 26 people there? Part of this refers to the third section below, the highly networked society of that time, and the even more highly networked church. Some of these people were business people who had travelled back and forth between other Christian centres: Corinth, Ephesus, and Rome. However, many are co-workers who Paul has worked with in other places and are now in Rome, or workers that he has heard about in Rome.

> *I commend to you our sister Phoebe, a deacon of the church in Cenchreae. I ask you to receive her in the Lord in a way worthy of his people and to give her any help she may need from you, for she has been the benefactor of many people, including me (vs 1-2).*

Phoebe was one of the leaders in the church in Corinth—perhaps in Rome on business, but probably tasked with carrying the letter.

> *Greet Priscilla and Aquila, my co-workers in Christ Jesus. They risked their lives for me. Not only I but*

---

[148] See *Dictionary of Paul and His Letters (The IVP Bible Dictionary Series)*, Gerald F. Hawthorne. (Published by IVP Academic, 1993).

all the churches of the Gentiles are grateful to them
(vs 3-4).

Paul had met this couple in Corinth, later took them to Ephesus, and now they are working in Rome.

Greet my dear friend Epenetus, who was the first
convert to Christ in the province of Asia (v 5).

This was a person converted in Turkey, presently living in Rome, but still connected. It is unclear whether he moved there for business or ministry.

Greet Mary, who worked very hard for you. Greet
Andronicus and Junia, my fellow Jews who have been
in prison with me. They are outstanding among the
apostles, and they were in Christ before I was . . .
Greet Urbanus, our co-worker in Christ, and my dear
friend Stachys . . . Greet Tryphena and Tryphosa,
those women who work hard in the Lord. Greet my
dear friend Persis, another woman who has worked
very hard in the Lord (vs 6-7; 9, 12).

Note the references to people who Paul knows are working hard in the work of God.

Greet Rufus, chosen in the Lord, and his mother, who
has been a mother to me, too (v 13).

Greet Asyncritus, Phlegon, Hermes, Patrobas,
Hermas and the brothers and sisters with them (v 14).

Greet Philologus, Julia, Nereus and his sister, and
Olympas and all the Lord's people who are with them
(v 15).

As Paul finishes his greetings he includes greetings from other Christians in Corinth to these people in Rome.

Timothy, my co-worker, sends his greetings to you,

as do Lucius, Jason and Sosipater, my fellow Jews. I, Tertius, who wrote down this letter, greet you in the Lord. Gaius, whose hospitality I and the whole church here enjoy, sends you his greetings. Erastus, who is the city's director of public works, and our brother Quartus send you their greetings (vs 21-23).

Corinthians

This is an extraordinary sense of connection and intentional fostering of relationship between churches and among co-workers in the network of churches. They were one family.

When Timothy comes, see to it that he has nothing to fear while he is with you, for he is carrying on the work of the Lord, just as I am. No one, then, should treat him with contempt (1 Cor. 16:10-11).

Paul is aware of coworkers moving between churches and wants to facilitate this process.

I was glad when Stephanas, Fortunatus and Achaicus arrived, because they have supplied what was lacking from you (v 17).

So this church had sent a team to Paul.

Aquila and Priscilla greet you warmly in the Lord, and so does the church that meets at their house (v 19b).

Here is the couple who was in Corinth and now are involved in ministry in another city because they had accompanied Paul in his move there.[149]

Tychicus, the dear brother and faithful servant in the

---

[149] See Acts 18:18.

Lord, will tell you everything, so that you also may know how I am and what I am doing. I am sending him to you for this very purpose, that you may know how we are, and that he may encourage you (Eph. 6:21-22).

This is the first of five references to Paul intentionally and strategically sending one person from one church to visit another church. Paul as apostle says, "I am sending him to you." This is about the grace on Paul's life to bless churches through sending other ministries he knows will benefit them and meet needs they have.

Philippians

The references to others are spread throughout Philippians rather than concentrated at the end.

I hope in the Lord Jesus to send Timothy to you soon, that I also may be cheered when I receive news about you (2:19).

Here is a second reference to Paul sending someone.

But I think it is necessary to send back to you Epaphroditus, my brother, co-worker and fellow soldier, who is also your messenger, whom you sent to take care of my needs. For he longs for all of you and is distressed because you heard he was ill. Indeed he was ill, and almost died. But God had mercy on him, and not on him only but also on me, to spare me sorrow upon sorrow. Therefore I am all the more eager to send him, so that when you see him again you may be glad and I may have less anxiety. So then, welcome him in the Lord with great joy, and honor people like him, because he almost died for the work

*of Christ. He risked his life to make up for the help
you yourselves could not give me (vs 25-30).*

Here is a second example of someone who had been sent by a
church to support Paul.

*Moreover, as you Philippians know, in the early days
of your acquaintance with the gospel, when I set out
from Macedonia, not one church shared with me in
the matter of giving and receiving, except you only;
for even when I was in Thessalonica, you sent me aid
more than once when I was in need. Not that I desire
your gifts, what I desire is that more be credited to
your account. I have received full payment and have
more than enough; I am amply supplied, now that I
have received from Epaphroditus the gifts you sent.
They are a fragrant offering, an acceptable sacrifice,
pleasing to God (4:15-18).*

Here a church sent people to support Paul's apostolic ministry—
people and money.

*Greet all God's people in Christ Jesus. The brothers
and sisters who are with me send greetings. All God's
people here send you greetings, especially those who
belong to Caesar's household (vs 21-22).*

Colossians and Others

Although Paul does not name co-workers here, he shows how he
seeks to establish links through greetings.

*Tychicus will tell you all the news about me. He is a
dear brother, a faithful minister and fellow servant
in the Lord. I am sending him to you for the express
purpose that you may know about our circumstances
and that he may encourage your hearts. He is coming
with Onesimus, our faithful and dear brother, who*

is one of you. They will tell you everything that is happening here (Col. 4:7-9).

In verse 8, Paul for a third time speaks of sending someone—"I am sending him to you"—and the church was to receive him as someone sent by Paul. He also sent back with him someone, Onesimus, who had come from that church.

My fellow prisoner Aristarchus sends you his greetings, as does Mark, the cousin of Barnabas. (You have received instructions about him; if he comes to you, welcome him.) Jesus, who is called Justus, also sends greetings. These are the only Jews among my co-workers for the kingdom of God, and they have proved a comfort to me. Epaphras, who is one of you and a servant of Christ Jesus, sends greetings. He is always wrestling in prayer for you, that you may stand firm in all the will of God, mature and fully assured. I vouch for him that he is working hard for you and for those at Laodicea and Hierapolis (vs 10-13).

Again here is an example of someone from that church who is now based with Paul in another church but still praying for the first church. The final statement about "working hard for you" suggests he had been sent from that church to help Paul.

Our dear friend Luke, the doctor, and Demas send greetings. Give my greetings to the brothers at Laodicea, and to Nympha and the church in her house. After this letter has been read to you, see that it is also read in the church of the Laodiceans and that you in turn read the letter from Laodicea. Tell Archippus: "See to it that you complete the ministry you have received in the Lord" (vs 14-17).

Paul fosters interconnections between churches, and sees himself as ministering to a network where letters are exchanged. He also knows the church well enough to have a prophetic word of encouragement for a member there that he knows by name and he obviously knows something of that person's life and ministry.

> *We sent Timothy, who is our brother and God's co-worker in God's service in spreading the gospel of Christ, to strengthen and encourage you in your faith (1 Thess. 3:2).*

Here is a fourth reference to Paul sending someone to be a blessing to a church he knew.

> *Greet Priscilla and Aquila and the household of Onesiphorus. Erastus stayed in Corinth, and I left Trophimus sick in Miletus. Do your best to get here before winter. Eubulus greets you, and so do Pudens, Linus, Claudia and all the brothers and sisters (2 Tim. 4:19-21).*

Here Paul requests that Timothy come to him to assist him. Paul has in his thinking a range of coworkers in various locations.

> *As soon as I send Artemas or Tychicus to you, do your best to come to me at Nicopolis, because I have decided to winter there. Do everything you can to help Zenas the lawyer and Apollos on their way and see that they have everything they need (Titus 3:12-13).*

Here is a fifth instance of Paul sending someone—this time moving ministries around strategically. Paul repositions ministries around the churches.

We see a picture of a lot of movement back and forwards between churches. As we reflect on implications, the thing that strikes me is that this was not purely relational and collegial, but Paul exercised a strategic intentional role. He built connections between churches and ministries but he also strategically sent people to different locations to help the churches there, and churches sent people to assist what Paul was doing.

New Testament Scholars and a Picture of the Early Church

In 1998, a book was published, *The Gospel for all Christians: Rethinking the Gospel Audiences,*[150] dealing with a fairly technical academic issue in New Testament studies about the Gospels, and countering the idea that they were written to address the specific issues of one community. The authors seek to show that the Gospels were actually intended to be circulated to a wider network of churches. What is interesting and relevant on a more general level is the picture they show of the early church as highly networked.

In the introduction Richard Bauckham states:

> *Of great importance is the extensive evidence that the early Christian movement was not . . . a scattering of relatively isolated, introverted communities, but a network of communities in constant, close communication with each other.*

Imagine saying that of the Vision network of churches: "The Vision network is not a scattering of relatively isolated, introverted communities, but a network of communities in constant, close communication with each other." Constant . . . and close . . . communication. This network thing is far stronger, far more powerful, and far more organic than we have realised.

Bauckham then goes on to say:

> *All the evidence we have for early Christian leaders . . . shows them to have been typically people*

---

[150] Edited by Richard Bauckham.

*who travelled widely and worked in more than one
community at different times.*

Leaders served a network of churches, not just developed their
own ministry in one church.

Summarising the communities and the leaders, he says:

*Both had a strong, lively and informed sense of
participation in a worldwide movement.*

They saw themselves not just as part of a local church but as
part of a dynamic network of churches all around the Mediterranean.
They knew people in other churches, they regularly travelled back and
forth between churches, they invested in the development of other
churches, and people were repositioned around the network for the
strategic development of the network.

Bauckham goes on to explain this in terms of the Roman Empire.

*The first thing this information tells us is that mobility
and communication in first century Roman world
were exceptionally high. Unprecedentedly good
roads and unprecedentedly safe travel by both land
and sea made the Mediterranean world of this time
more closely interconnected than any large area of
the ancient world had ever been. People travelled
on business as merchants, traders and bankers, on
pilgrimage to religious festivals, in search of health
and healing at the healing shrines and spas, to
consult the oracles which flourished in this period, to
attend the pan-Hellenic games and the various lesser
versions of these all over the empire, as soldiers in the
legions, as government personnel of many kinds and
even on vacation and as sightseers. . . . It was certainly
not only the wealthy who travelled. Quite ordinary
people travelled to healing shrines, religious festivals*

and games. . . . Therefore, people quite typical of the members of the early Christian churches regularly travelled.

The world has never been as similar to this era as it is today. We also live in a globally connected world, but this time our sense of connection and our capability for connection is massively increased through technology—24/7 live news coverage, wifi, video call apps, email, smartphones, inexpensive travel and acccomodations, international conferences, multinational companies, international sport events, world travel tourism, etc.

However, Bauckham notes another factor for Christians.

But in addition to Christian participation in the ordinary mobility of society, much communication was deliberately fostered between the churches.

There was another dimension of intentional networking above and beyond the everyday movements of a mobile society. Bauckham lists references to early leaders moving around: Polycarp, Bishop of Smyrna, visited Rome and Syria. Abercius, Bishop of Hierapolis (in Turkey), travelled West to Rome, and East to Syria. Bauckham says:

Other prominent second century teachers seem almost as a rule, to have taught for a time in more than one major Christian centre.

His summary is:

It seems that leaders who moved from church to church, to a greater or lesser extent, are a constant feature of the early Christian movement in the first century and a half of its existence.

One author, Michael Thompson, has a chapter in the book called, *The Holy Internet: Communication between Churches in the*

First Christian Generation.[151] He uses the picture of the Internet to describe how the early church functioned. He first considers the paths of communication.

> *In the ancient world the closest thing to an information superhighway was the grid of Roman roads and clear shipping lanes that made travel far safer and easier than it had ever been before.*

He points out that though there was no public postal service, the Empire depended on a regular secure system of communication that included staging posts and rest stops when towns were separated by more than one day's journey.

Secondly, he then considers the "archives of information":

> *"The network 'servers' of the holy internet were the churches" and he notes the importance of "hubs": Jerusalem, Antioch, Ephesus, Corinth, and Rome. These functioned as hubs for the surrounding areas. Paul seems to have focused on establishing new hubs of the network, which then networked into the surrounding areas (now there's a thought of strategic importance!).*

Thirdly, he considers the access to the Internet. Staying with the Internet metaphor, he says communication depended on the "protocol software of hospitality." There is extensive writing in the early church on expectations of hospitality towards Christians, and specifically, travelling Christians in ministry. Comments, like in the early Christian writing, the Didache, that visitors were to be freely extended hospitality for two to three days but after that they needed to move on or work, and if they asked for an offering, they were certainly

---

[151] Thompson, Michael B. *The Holy Internet: Communication Between Churches in the First Christian Generation.* (Published by T&T Clark, 1997).

to be rejected as false prophets! I realise the pendulum has swung to "honouring" visiting ministry, and people being worth their labour, and churches being stretched to have faith, but maybe we need to also rediscover another simpler model of travelling ministries being hosted in homes, and ministry as service to the network of churches.

Finally, Thompson has some interesting analysis of the speed of this "Internet". Remember travel was generally by walking or by ship: Jerusalem to Antioch took 8-10 days, on to Ephesus was another 14-30 days by sea, or 35 days over land. Ephesus to Corinth, 6-10 days; Corinth to Rome, 10-25 days. From Rome directly back to Jerusalem by sea, 16-28 days. In our modern era of email, cellphones, and air travel, it is mindboggling to consider how the early church managed to be so highly networked in spite of their many obstacles and challenges.

How can we be less highly networked than they were? They obviously put a high value on being part of a dynamic network of churches.

Implications

What strikes me about this picture? Three points stand out.

Firstly, they viewed themselves as part of one network of churches. People knew each other, they regularly travelled back and forth between churches and ministries, and they regularly moved around the network. *The focus was on the health and development of the whole network—actually the value and blessing and joy was being part of the whole network.*

Secondly, there is a sense of intentional networking, and even more so, strategic networking directed by the apostolic leadership. For example, Paul would send a worker to another church because he believed this was significant for the development and health of the receiving church.

Thirdly, churches sent people and resources to partner with and support Paul in the initiatives he was undertaking. I suspect they saw him in his apostolic ministry as something of the spearhead or cutting edge of the development of the network. *Combining the last two, apostolic leadership was welcomed, received, and invested in through sending support (people and money) to what Paul, as an apostle, was investing in, and he in turn deployed people for the development of the network.*

Now just to earth all this, without seeking to either copy or react, we can be provoked by the example of Equippers. There is an Equippers church in Christchurch, and I notice that every few weeks there seems to be a speaker from another Equippers' church. After pastoring a small church I must confess I wonder how they do it. When our church was small, we had a budget for visiting ministry of maybe $600 per year, which meant, maybe one out-of-town visit and a couple of local visits. Even as a medium-size church the budget was maybe $1,200, which with the culture of increased payments, did not really go much further! *One question is how do we make networking viable particularly for smaller churches?*

Two Practical Steps

Firstly, while I can be intentional in developing my connections, I understand that there is a dimension to the network of Nick knowing the needs of various churches, and making strategic decisions to send ministries to churches. Bearing in mind the financial constraints of some smaller churches, I thought one thing I could do would be to say to Nick, "I cannot afford to give a lot of money to the network, but I can give my time. So I would like to give two Sundays/weekends per year to you that you could send me wherever you want, and there would be no expectation of payment or offering—they can give me a box of chocolates or a cheese board, if they want! This would be seen as the network investing in the church, and for me, this would be part of my service to the network." If a number of us did something like that, it would empower the network, and empower Nick to be strategic in developing the network.

Secondly, I thought there could be someone God has blessed with resources and who has prospered, and they might like to create a fund initially of perhaps $5,000 per year that allowed Nick to say, "We need to invest in Whangarei this year, so Trevor, I want to send you there in April, and Michael, I want to send you there in August, and we will cover your airfares."

These two steps—people offering time to invest in churches based on an expectation of hospitality and without expecting extra payment (others offering money to create a fund to cover travel)—would enable some strategic intentional "sending," above and beyond the collegial or peer relational connections and invitations that continue to develop.

It all starts, though, when we see that the puzzle is the network, and my ministry is one piece of the jigsaw puzzle of the network, and even more when we begin to feel how liberating, empowering, safe, and exciting it would feel to find where my ministry fits within the network.

Having A Multiplication Mindset

Beware! This is not for the faint-hearted!

Having read through *Multiplication*, my hope is that you agree it's a good thing to plant churches that plant churches. By now you will have also realised that I've been personally arrested and disturbed by the concept of Multiplication—churches planting churches that plant churches. Instead of planting one tree, they plant a forest—in fact, *forests*. I confess that early on, I missed Jesus' divine strategy: Multiplication. I now see this is God's passion and purpose. Where we've been addicted to addition, prioritising the gathering, and urging people to "come," the commission, priority, and emphasis of Jesus all along has been, "Go."

The following are some thoughts about the nature of those with a Multiplication Mindset (MM) who are characteristically marked by and passionately adhere to these attributes. They assume that lost people really matter to God, and as such, "MMs" are always praying and thinking about how they can reach just one more person for Jesus.

What Characterises a MM Person?

1. They understand discipleship is *the* key. It's the number 1 priority to Multiplication, and it is what Jesus commanded us to do.

They ask: "Who is discipling you?" and "Who are you discipling?" Leaders of MM churches are interested in how many are being apprenticed, and how many apprentices are leading in mission.

2. They don't look at the attendance size of the church before they plant church-planting churches. Their criteria is leader readiness.

3. A church often says: "WE can do it. You can help." MMs say: "YOU can do it! We can help." This church realises the priesthood of *all* believers: From volunteer, to a person who is called to serve. MMs ask: "How can we empower more people to be involved in Kingdom activity?" People in MM churches don't ask, "Am I called to ministry?" They ask, "What is the ministry God called me to?"

4. The MM person says, "Let's pastor the city, not just our own church."

5. The MM person says: Sending capacity is the focus, not seating capacity.

6. The MM person develops an apostolic atmosphere, an apostolic culture. This is a high priority. An apostolic culture is one that focusses on sending and releasing people.

7. The MM person asks: "Does the mission have a church?", not "Does the church have a mission?" They are open to new ways of thinking, new ideas, and are ready to discuss possibilities.

8. The MM person has a "yes"-attitude. It doesn't have a bias to a no-attitude.

9. The MM person has a minimalist theology about what church is. It does not in any way water down the truth of Scripture or its priority. It simply wrestles with, "What is church for us?"

10. The MM person is about planting church-planting churches. This results in new networks and movements of churches.

11. The MM person says, "Let's give a significant percentage of finance for church-planting churches." (Minimal is 10%.)

12. The MM person focusses on releasing people and ministries

before prioritising bigger buildings. Here's a radical thought: Are you willing to make church multiplication a higher priority than church facilities? If you are not in a building yet, are you willing to plant your first church before building your first building?

13. The MM person understands that local churches are the key drivers to begetting churches. Central vision is good but lacks greatness. A defining aspect of Multiplication is churches beginning new churches. Local churches take responsibility and ownership for planting churches.

Todd Wilson, from Exponential, writes:

> *The prevailing value we place on accumulation is at the core of why less than 4 percent of U.S. churches ever reproduce (or why greater than 96 percent of churches never reproduce). Ponder the consequences of less than 4 percent of adults ever having children.*
>
> *Lately, however, I've been encouraged that an increasing number of church leaders are becoming discontented with the elusive, addition-focused scorecard that never satisfies. These leaders are wrestling with redefining their success—shifting their focus and behaviors from attracting and accumulating to releasing and sending. They get that our "sentness" is at the heart of Kingdom multiplication and the fruit of biblical disciple-making.*[152]

I believe he makes an important point. What do you think?

In Europe, particularly, MM people are nearly non-existent. Yet I am absolutely convinced the ONLY way to reach the nations of Europe in a harvest is with an Multiplication Mindset.

The following are questions to activate and advance you into a position of leader readiness with a Multiplication Mindset.

---

[152] Exponential newsletter email, Feb. 2017.

REFLECTION

1. Which Multiplication Mindsets (MMs) speak to you? In what way do they speak to you, and how do they challenge you?

_____

_____

_____

_____

_____

_____

_____

2. What action steps could you implement to begin now?

_____

_____

_____

3. What do you think about what Todd Wilson says?

_____

_____

_____

_____

4. Which MMs do you feel you are functioning in?

_____

_____

_____

In what way?

_____

_____

_____

5. What MMs can you put into action over the next year? –The next 3-5 years?

_____

_____

_____

_____

_____

6. If you are part of a church leadership team, how could you get others in a conversation regarding MMs?

_____

_____

_____

_____

ABOUT THE AUTHOR

NICK KLINKENBERG, and his wife, Karen, are passionate about the local church, the multiplication of churches, seeing people come to Christ, and seeing God move in signs, wonders, and miracles. Nick has been in church and movement leadership roles for over thirty-five years. Founder of Vision Churches International, Nick travels locally and abroad, especially in Europe. He facilitates and oversees the pioneering of new churches, networks, and movements, as well as coaching and encouraging leaders.

Nick and his wife are commissioned by, and partner with *C3 Churches - Global.* Nick is the author of *Daily Medicine* and co-author of *Miracles in Aotearoa NZ.*

Nick and Karen have raised three sons and have six grandchildren.

Attendance   —
Buildings   —
Cash   —
Programs   —

Performance   —
Professionalism .

$\underline{\frac{V}{=}}$

Lost.
Presence.
People.
Mission.
Planning.

RESOURCES

DAILY MEDICINE FROM HIS WORD (Book)

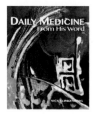

One chapter for every day of the month. These 31 short chapters will nurture and empower you to believe God for all you need. Each day focusses on healing Scriptures and thoughts, and provides space for your notes. *Daily Medicine* is a great way to build your faith as you read and meditate on His Word each day.

MIRACLES IN AOTEAROA NZ (Book)

Hundreds of testimonies from New Zealand healing evangelist, Weston Carryer. Over 600 pages of phenomenal testimonies showing Jesus' healing power over all kinds of sickness and disease. This book is a faith-builder that will encourage you.

For more information, and to read our blogs about church planting and leadership, visit our websites:

www.nickklinkenberg.com

www.visionchurches.com